The Tree of Liberty

By Anthony Blandino

Dedicated to our fellow independent
American thinkers.

Table of Contents

I
ON FREEDOM & DEFENSE

"We hold these truths to be self-evident: that all men are created equal; that they are endowed by their Creator with certain unalienable rights; that among these are life, liberty, and the pursuit of happiness."- Thomas Jefferson

FILIPPO MAZZEI
December 25, 1730 - March 19, 1816

"All men are by nature equally free and independent. Such equality is necessary in order to create a free government. All men must be equal to each other in natural law."

BENJAMIN FRANKLIN
January 17, 1706 - April 17, 1790

"The Constitution only gives people the right to pursue happiness. You have to catch it yourself."

"Distrust and caution are the parents of security."

"Where liberty is, there is my country."

"Three can keep a secret, if two of them are dead."

"They who can give up essential liberty to obtain a little temporary safety deserve neither liberty nor safety."

"We must, indeed, all hang together or, most assuredly, we shall all hang separately."

"Words may show a man's wit but actions his meaning."

PATRICK HENRY
May 29, 1736 - June 6, 1799

"Guard with jealous attention the public liberty. Suspect everyone who approaches that jewel. Unfortunately, nothing will preserve it but downright force. Whenever you give up that force, you are inevitably ruined."

"Is life so dear or peace so sweet as to be purchased at the price of chains and slavery? Forbid it, Almighty God! I know not what course others may take, but as for me, give me liberty, or give me death!"

"Are we at last brought to such humiliating and debasing degradation, that we cannot be trusted with arms for our defense?"

"The great object is that every man be armed."

"The liberties of a people never were, nor ever will be, secure, when the transactions of their rulers may be concealed from them."

"Perfect freedom is as necessary to the health and vigor of commerce as it is to the health and vigor of citizenship."

"If this be treason, make the most of it!"

ALEXANDER HAMILTON
January 11, 1755 - July 12, 1804

"Safety from external danger is the most powerful director of national conduct. Even the ardent love of liberty will, after a time, give way to its dictates."

"Power over a man's subsistence is power over his will."

"The nation which can prefer disgrace to danger is prepared for a master and deserves one."

GEORGE WASHINGTON
February 22, 1732 - December 14, 1799

"Experience teaches us that it is much easier to prevent an enemy from posting themselves than it is to dislodge them after they have got possession."

"If we desire to avoid insult, we must be able to repel it; if we desire to secure peace, one of the most powerful instruments of our rising prosperity, it must be known, that we are at all times ready for War."

"The time is near at hand which must determine whether Americans are to be free men or slaves."

"Guard against the impostures of pretended patriotism."

"Liberty, when it begins to take root, is a plant of rapid growth."

"When we assumed the Soldier, we did not lay aside the Citizen."

"The constitution vests the power of declaring war in Congress; therefore no offensive expedition of importance can be undertaken until after they shall have deliberated upon the subject and authorized such a measure."

"I can only say that there is not a man living who wishes more sincerely than I do, to see a plan adopted for the abolition of it - but there is only one proper and effectual mode by which it can be accomplished, and that is by

Legislative authority: and this, as far as my suffrage will go, shall never be wanting.

"Nothing can be more hurtful to the service, than the neglect of discipline; for that discipline, more than numbers, gives one army the superiority over another."

"Discipline is the soul of an army. It makes small numbers formidable; procures success to the weak, and esteem to all."

"My first wish is to see this plague of mankind, war, banished from the earth."

"I walk on untrodden ground. There is scarcely any part of my conduct which may not hereafter be drawn into precedent.

ABIGAIL ADAMS
November 22, 1744 - October 28, 1818

"Arbitrary power is like most other things which are very hard, very liable to be broken."- Abigail Adams

"We have too many high-sounding words, and too few actions that correspond with them."

"If particular care and attention is not paid to the ladies, we are determined to foment a rebellion, and will not hold ourselves bound by any laws in which we have no voice, or representation."

"Great necessities call out great virtues."

HENRY KNOX
July 25, 1750 - October 25, 1806

"We have arrived at that point of time in which we are forced to see our own humiliation, as a nation, and that a progression in this line cannot be a productive of happiness, private or public."

"Something is wanting, and something must be done, or we shall be involved in all the horror of failure, and civil war without a prospect of its termination."

"Every friend to the liberty of his country is bound to reflect, and step forward to prevent the dreadful consequences which shall result from a government of events."

NATHAN HALE
June 6, 1755 - September 22, 1776

"I only regret that I have but one life to lose for my country."

"It is the duty of every good officer to obey any orders given him by his commander in chief."

"I greatly fear some of America's greatest and most dangerous enemies are such as think themselves her best friends."

NOAH WEBSTER
October 16, 1758 - May 28, 1843

"When a citizen gives his suffrage to a man of known immorality he abuses his trust; he sacrifices not only his own interest, but that of his neighbor; he betrays the interest of his country."

THOMAS PAINE
February 9, 1737 - June 8, 1809

"If there must be trouble, let it be in my day, that my child may have peace."

"The harder the conflict, the more glorious the triumph."

"Arms discourage and keep the invader and plunderer in awe, and preserve order in the world as well as property... Horrid mischief would ensue were the law-abiding deprived of the use of them."

"The strength and power of despotism consists wholly in the fear of resistance."

"He that would make his own liberty secure, must guard even his enemy from oppression; for if he violates this duty, he establishes a precedent that will reach to himself."

"These are the times that try men's souls."

JOHN PAUL JONES
July 6, 1747 - July 18, 1792

"I have not yet begun to fight!"- John Paul Jones

"It seems to be a law of nature, inflexible and inexorable, that those who will not risk cannot win."

"I wish to have no connection with any ship that does not sail fast; for I intend to go in harm's way."

"An honorable peace is and always was my first wish! I can take no delight in the effusion of human blood; but, if this war should continue, I wish to have the most active part in it."

"Whoever can surprise well must conquer."

SAMUEL ADAMS
September 27, 1722 - October 2, 1803

"The Constitution shall never be construed... to prevent the people of the United States who are peaceable citizens from keeping their own arms."

"The liberties of our country, the freedom of our civil constitution, are worth defending against all hazards: And it is our duty to defend them against all attacks."

"Our contest is not only whether we ourselves shall be free, but whether there shall be left to mankind an asylum on earth for civil and religious liberty."

"The natural liberty of man is to be free from any superior power on Earth, and not to be under the will or legislative authority of man, but only to have the law of nature for his rule."

"Among the natural rights of the colonists are these: First a right to life, secondly to liberty, and thirdly to property; together with the right to defend them in the best manner they can."

JAMES MADISON
March 16, 1751 - June 28, 1836

"The personal right to acquire property, which is a natural right, gives to property, when acquired, a right to protection, as a social right."

"The class of citizens, who provide at once their own food and their own raiment, may be viewed as the most truly independent and happy."

"Americans have the right and advantage of being armed - unlike the citizens of other countries whose governments are afraid to trust the people with arms."

"A well regulated militia, composed of the body of the people, trained in arms, is the best most natural defense of a free country."

"Despotism can only exist in darkness, and there are too many lights now in the political firmament to permit it to remain anywhere, as it has heretofore done, almost everywhere."

"If Tyranny and Oppression come to this land, it will be in the guise of fighting a foreign enemy."

"The people are the only legitimate fountain of power, and it is from them that the constitutional charter, under which the several branches of government hold their power, is derived."

"Of all the enemies of public liberty, war is perhaps the most to be dreaded, because it comprises and develops the germ of every other."

"No nation could preserve its freedom in the midst of continual warfare."

JOHN ADAMS
October 30, 1735 - July 4, 1826

"Property is surely a right of mankind as real as liberty."

"The fundamental law of the militia is that it be created, directed and commanded by the laws, and ever for the support of the laws."

"Democracy... while it lasts is more bloody than either aristocracy or monarchy. Remember, democracy never lasts long. It soon wastes, exhausts, and murders itself. There is never a democracy that did not commit suicide."

MERCY OTIS WARREN
September 25, 1728 - October 19, 1814

"The British were indeed very far superior to the Americans in every respect necessary to military operations, except the revivified courage and resolution, the result of sudden success after despair."

"Democratic principles are the result of equality of condition."

JAMES MONROE
April 28, 1758 - July 4, 1831

"It is only when the people become ignorant and corrupt, when they degenerate into a populace, that they are incapable of exercising their sovereignty."

"Our country may be likened to a new house. We lack many things, but we possess the most precious of all - liberty!"

THOMAS JEFFERSON
April 13, 1743 - July 4, 1826

"The tree of liberty must be refreshed from time to time with the blood of patriots and tyrants."

"Mankind are more disposed to suffer, while evils are sufferable, than to right themselves by abolishing the forms to which they are accustomed."

"None but an armed nation can dispense with a standing army. To keep ours armed and disciplined is therefore at all times important."

"We are not to expect to be translated from despotism to liberty in a featherbed."

"Timid men prefer the calm of despotism to the tempestuous sea of liberty."

"The spirit of resistance to government is so valuable on certain occasions that I wish it to be always kept alive."

"If a nation expects to be ignorant and free, in a state of civilization, it expects what never was and never will be."

"Leave no authority existing not responsible to the people."

"Force is the vital principle and immediate parent of despotism."

"Nothing is unchangeable but the inherent and unalienable rights of man."

"The boisterous sea of liberty is never without a wave."

"I would rather be exposed to the inconveniences attending too much liberty than those attending too small a degree of it."

"No freeman shall be debarred the use of arms."

"The constitutions of most of our States assert that all power is inherent in the people; that... it is their right and duty to be at all times armed."

"One loves to possess arms, though they hope never to have occasion for them."

"It is our duty still to endeavor to avoid war; but if it shall actually take place, no matter by whom brought on, we must defend ourselves. If our house be on fire, without inquiring whether it was fired from within or without, we must try to extinguish it."

"For a people who are free, and who mean to remain so, a well-organized and armed militia is their best security."

"Rightful liberty is unobstructed action according to our will within limits drawn around us by the equal rights of others. I do not add 'within the limits of the law' because law is often but the tyrant's will, and always so when it violates the rights of the individual."

"All, too, will bear in mind this sacred principle, that though the will of the majority is in all cases to prevail, that will to be rightful must be reasonable; that the minority possess their equal rights, which equal law must protect, and to violate would be oppression."

"The God who gave us life, gave us liberty at the same time."

"To compel a man to furnish funds for the propagation of ideas he disbelieves and abhors is sinful and tyrannical."

"Experience hath shewn, that even under the best forms of government those entrusted with power have, in time, and by slow operations, perverted it into tyranny."

"Our country is now taking so steady a course as to show by what road it will pass to destruction, to wit: by consolidation of power first, and then corruption, it's necessary consequence."

"A Bill of Rights is what the people are entitled to against every government, and what no just government should refuse, or rest on inference."

"We hold these truths to be self-evident: that all men are created equal; that they are endowed by their Creator with certain unalienable rights; that among these are life, liberty, and the pursuit of happiness."

ABRAHAM LINCOLN
February 12, 1809 - April 15, 1865

"Our Declaration of Independence was held sacred by all and thought to include all; but now, to aid in making the bondage of the Negro universal and eternal, it is assailed, sneered at, construed, hawked at, and torn, till, if its framers could rise from their graves, they could not at all recognize it."

"Let reverence for the laws be breathed by every American mother to the lisping babe that prattles on her lap - let it be taught in schools, in seminaries, and in colleges; let it be written in primers, spelling books, and in almanacs; let it be preached from the pulpit, proclaimed in legislative halls, and enforced in courts of justice."

"It was that which gave promise that in due time the weights should be lifted from the shoulders of all men, and that all should have an equal chance. This is the sentiment embodied in that Declaration of Independence."

"Be sure you put your feet in the right place, then stand firm.

"America will never be destroyed from the outside. If we falter and lose our freedoms, it will be because we destroyed ourselves."

"At what point then is the approach of danger to be expected? I answer, if it ever reach us, it must spring up amongst us. It cannot come from abroad. If destruction be our lot, we must ourselves be its author and finisher. As a nation of freemen, we must live through all time, or die by suicide."

"He who would be no slave must consent to have no slave. Those who deny freedom to others deserve it not for themselves and, under a just God, cannot long retain it."

"The people know their rights, and they are never slow to assert and maintain them when they are invaded."

"Gold is good in its place; but loving, brave, patriotic men are better than gold."

"Public sentiment is everything. With public sentiment, nothing can fail. Without it, nothing can succeed."

"I should like to know if, taking this old Declaration of Independence, which declares that all men are equal upon principle, you begin making exceptions to it, where will you stop? If one man says it does not mean a Negro, why not another say it does not mean some other man?"

"True patriotism is better than the wrong kind of piety."

"Standing as I do, with my hand upon this staff, and under the folds of the American flag, I ask you to stand by me so long as I stand by it."

"Stand with anybody that stands right, stand with him while he right and part with him when he goes wrong."

"I am not bound to win, but I am bound to be true. I am not bound to succeed, but I am bound to live by the light that I have. I must stand with anybody that stands right, and stand with him while he is right, and part with him when he goes wrong."

"The shepherd drives the wolf from the sheep for which the sheep thanks the shepherd as his liberator, while the wolf denounces him for the same act as the destroyer of liberty. Plainly, the sheep and the wolf are not agreed upon a definition of liberty."

"Our defense is in the preservation of the spirit which prizes liberty as a heritage of all men, in all lands, everywhere. Destroy this spirit and you have planted the seeds of despotism around your own garden."

"Any people anywhere, being inclined and having the power, have the right to rise up, and shake off the existing government, and form a new one that suits them better. This is a most valuable - a most sacred right - a right, which we hope and believe, is to liberate the world."

"This country, with its institutions, belongs to the people who inhabit it. Whenever they shall grow weary of the existing government, they can exercise their constitutional right of amending it, or exercise their revolutionary right to overthrow it."

"We the people are the rightful masters of both Congress and the courts, not to overthrow the Constitution but to overthrow the men who pervert the Constitution."

"My dream is of a place and a time where America will once again be seen as the last best hope of earth."

"No man is good enough to govern another man without the other's consent."

"Those who deny freedom to others deserve it not for themselves; and under the rule of a just God, cannot long retain it."

"As I would not be a slave, so I would not be a master. This expresses my idea of democracy.

"Four score and seven years ago our fathers brought forth on this continent, a new nation, conceived in Liberty, and dedicated to the proposition that all men are created equal."

"That we here highly resolve that these dead shall not have died in vain - that this nation, under God, shall have a new birth of freedom - and that government of the people, by the people, for the people, shall not perish from the earth."

HARRIET TUBMAN
c. March 1822 - March 10, 1913

"I freed a thousand slaves I could have freed a thousand more if only they knew they were slaves."

"I grew up like a neglected weed - ignorant of liberty, having no experience of it."

"Never wound a snake; kill it."

"I had crossed the line. I was free; but there was no one to welcome me to the land of freedom. I was a stranger in a strange land."

"I can't die but once."

"I had reasoned this out in my mind, there was one of two things I had a right to, liberty or death; if I could not have one, I would have the other."

"I would fight for my liberty so long as my strength lasted, and if the time came for me to go, the Lord would let them take me."

"You'll be free or die!

THEODORE 'TEDDY' ROOSEVELT
October 27, 1858 - January 6, 1919

"A vote is like a rifle; its usefulness depends upon the character of the user."

"The man who loves other countries as much as his own stands on a level with the man who loves other women as much as he loves his own wife."

"We can have no '50-50' allegiance in this country. Either a man is an American and nothing else, or he is not an American at all."

"The first requisite of a good citizen in this republic of ours is that he shall be able and willing to pull his own weight."

"Speak softly and carry a big stick; you will go far."

"A man who is good enough to shed his blood for the country is good enough to be given a square deal afterwards."

WILL ROGERS
November 4, 1879 - August 15, 1935

"Liberty doesn't work as well in practice as it does in speeches."

DWIGHT DAVID 'IKE' EISENHOWER
October 14, 1890 - March 28, 1969

"Only our individual faith in freedom can keep us free."

"If you want total security, go to prison. There you're fed, clothed, given medical care and so on. The only thing lacking... is freedom."

"There is nothing wrong with America that faith, love of freedom, intelligence, and energy of her citizens cannot cure.

ROBERT HEINLEIN
July 7, 1907 - May 8, 1988

"You can have peace. Or you can have freedom. Don't ever count on having both at once."

"When any government, or any church for that matter, undertakes to say to its subjects, This you may not read, this you must not see, this you are forbidden to know, the end result is tyranny and oppression no matter how holy the motives."

"An armed society is a polite society. Manners are good when one may have to back up his acts with his life."

"I am free because I know that I alone am morally responsible for everything I do. I am free, no matter what rules surround me. If I find them tolerable, I tolerate them; if I find them too obnoxious, I break them. I am free because I know that I alone am morally responsible for everything I do."

RONALD REAGAN
February 6, 1911 - June 5, 2004

"Freedom is never more than one generation away from extinction. We didn't pass it to our children in the bloodstream. It must be fought for, protected, and handed on for them to do the same."

"If we love our country, we should also love our countrymen."

"Let us be sure that those who come after will say of us in our time, that in our time we did everything that could be done. We finished the race; we kept them free; we kept the faith."

"We will always remember. We will always be proud. We will always be prepared, so we will always be free."

"Trust, but verify."

"Mr. Gorbachev, tear down this wall!"

RICHARD NIXON
January 9, 1913 - April 22, 1994

"Americans admire a people who can scratch a desert and produce a garden. The Israelis have shown qualities that Americans identify with: guts, patriotism, idealism, a passion for freedom. I have seen it. I know. I believe that."

JOHN FITZGERALD KENNEDY
May 29, 1917 - November 22, 1963

"Let every nation know, whether it wishes us well or ill, that we shall pay any price, bear any burden, meet any hardship, support any friend, oppose any foe to assure the survival and the success of liberty."

"The cost of freedom is always high, but Americans have always paid it. And one path we shall never choose, and that is the path of surrender, or submission."

"Conformity is the jailer of freedom and the enemy of growth."

BILLY GRAHAM
November 7, 1918

"Freedom is relative."

"Once you've lost your privacy, you realize you've lost an extremely valuable thing."

ROBERT KENNEDY
November 20, 1925 - June 6, 1968

"The free way of life proposes ends, but it does not prescribe means."

MARTIN LUTHER KING JR.
January 15, 1929 - April 4, 1968

"Oppressed people cannot remain oppressed forever. The yearning for freedom eventually manifests itself."

"A right delayed is a right denied."

"Freedom is never voluntarily given by the oppressor; it must be demanded by the oppressed."

RON PAUL
August 20, 1935

"There is only one kind of freedom and that's individual liberty. Our lives come from our Creator and our liberty comes from our Creator. It has nothing to do with government granting it."

"Real patriotism is a willingness to challenge the government when it's wrong."

"Our country's founders cherished liberty, not democracy."

"I am just absolutely convinced that the best formula for giving us peace and preserving the American way of life is freedom, limited government, and minding our own business overseas."

GEORGE CARLIN
May 12, 1937 - June 22, 2008

"I think people should be allowed to do anything they want. We haven't tried that for a while. Maybe this time it'll work."

"Well, if crime fighters fight crime and fire fighters fight fire, what do freedom fighters fight? They never mention that part to us, do they?"

BEN CARSON
September 18, 1951

"I'm very hopeful that I'm not the only one who's willing to pick up the baton of freedom, because freedom is not free, and we must fight for it every day. Every one of us must fight for it, because we're fighting for our children and the next generation."

RAND PAUL
January 7, 1963

"There comes a time in the history of nations when fear and forgetfulness cause a nation to hesitate, to waver, and perhaps even to succumb. When that time comes, those who love liberty must rise to the occasion. Will you lovers of liberty rise to the occasion?"

"People say America is exceptional. I agree, but it's not the complexion of our skin or the twists in our DNA that make us unique. America is exceptional because we were founded upon the notion that everyone should be free to pursue life, liberty, and happiness."

"We must always embrace individual liberty and enforce the constitutional rights of all Americans-rich and poor, immigrant and native, black and white."

"If our freedom is taken, the American dream will wither and die."

"The sacrifice of our personal liberty for security is and will forever be a false choice."

"Freedom is popular. Bring it on."

"Whether you breach the Fourth Amendment 20 percent of the time or 100 percent of the time, it's still not the point. The point is whether or not you still collect millions of people's information with a single warrant."

"The NSA should keep close watch on suspected terrorists to keep our country safe - through programs permitting due process, the naming of a suspect, and oversight by an accountable court."

"The right to life is guaranteed to all Americans in the Declaration of Independence, and ensuring this is upheld is the Constitutional duty of all members of Congress."

TED CRUZ
December 22, 1970

"The power of the American people, when we rise up and stand for liberty, knows no bounds."

"It has been suggested that those of us who are fighting to defend liberty - fighting to turn around the out-of-control spending and out-of-control debt in this country, fighting to defend the Constitution, it has been suggested that we are wacko birds (Wacko birds comment by Senator John McCain)."

"My touchstone for every question is the Constitution."

"The Second Amendment is an integral part of the Bill of Rights."

"We are seeing a great awakening. A national movement of We the People, brought together by what unites us - a shared love of liberty, and an understanding of the unlimited potential of free men and free women."

THOMAS SOWELL
June 30, 1930

"Freedom has cost too much blood and agony to be relinquished at the cheap price of rhetoric."

"As for gun control advocates, I have no hope whatever that any facts whatever will make the slightest dent in their thinking - or lack of thinking."

JOHN WAYNE
May 26, 1907 - June 11, 1979

"All I'm for is the liberty of the individual"

CLINT EASTWOOD
May 31, 1930

"I have a very strict gun control policy: if there's a gun around, I want to be in control of it."

II
ON GOVERNMENT & SOCIETY

"Government, even in its best state, is but a necessary evil; in its worst state, an intolerable one."- Thomas Paine

ALEXANDER HAMILTON
January 11, 1755 - July 12, 1804

"Constitutions should consist only of general provisions; the reason is that they must necessarily be permanent, and that they cannot calculate for the possible change of things."

"In framing a government which is to be administered by men over men, the great difficulty lies in this: you must first enable the government to control the governed; and in the next place, oblige it to control itself."

"Even to observe neutrality you must have a strong government."

"A national debt, if it is not excessive, will be to us a national blessing."

"Why has government been instituted at all? Because the passions of man will not conform to the dictates of reason and justice without constraint."

"It's not tyranny we desire; it's a just, limited, federal government."

"Real liberty is neither found in despotism or the extremes of democracy, but in moderate governments."

"Unless your government is respectable, foreigners will invade your rights; and to maintain tranquility, it must be respectable - even to observe neutrality, you must have a strong government."

GEORGE WASHINGTON
February 22, 1732 - December 14, 1799

"Overgrown military establishments are under any form of government inauspicious to liberty, and are to be regarded as particularly hostile to republican liberty."

"The basis of our political system is the right of the people to make and to alter their constitutions of government."

"It will be found an unjust and unwise jealousy to deprive a man of his natural liberty upon the supposition he may abuse it."

"Observe good faith and justice toward all nations. Cultivate peace and harmony with all."

"Laws made by common consent must not be trampled on by individuals."

"The alternate domination of one faction over another, sharpened by the spirit of revenge natural to party dissension, which in different ages and countries has perpetrated the most horrid enormities, is itself a frightful despotism. But this leads at length to a more formal and permanent despotism."

"Arbitrary power is most easily established on the ruins of liberty abused to licentiousness."

"My observation is that whenever one person is found adequate to the discharge of a duty... it is worse executed by two persons, and scarcely done at all if three or more are employed therein."

"I have no other view than to promote the public good, and am unambitious of honors not founded in the approbation of my Country."

"The Constitution is the guide which I never will abandon."

ABIGAIL ADAMS
November 22, 1744 - October 28, 1818

"I am more and more convinced that man is a dangerous creature and that power, whether vested in many or a few, is ever grasping, and like the grave, cries, 'Give, give.'"

JOHN HANCOCK
January 23, 1737 - October 8, 1793

"The important consequences to the American States from this Declaration of Independence, considered as the ground and foundation of a future government, naturally suggest the propriety of proclaiming it in such a manner as that the people may be universally informed of it."

NOAH WEBSTER
October 16, 1758 - May 28, 1843

"No truth is more evident to my mind than that the Christian religion must be the basis of any government intended to secure the rights and privileges of a free people."

THOMAS PAINE
February 9, 1737 - June 8, 1809

"Government, even in its best state, is but a necessary evil; in its worst state, an intolerable one."

"Those who want to reap the benefits of this great nation must bear the fatigue of supporting it."

"It is the direction and not the magnitude which is to be taken into consideration."

"The instant formal government is abolished, society begins to act. A general association takes place, and common interest produces common security."

JAMES MADISON
March 16, 1751 - June 28, 1836

"Do not separate text from historical background. If you do, you will have perverted and subverted the Constitution, which can only end in a distorted, bastardized form of illegitimate government."

"The diversity in the faculties of men, from which the rights of property originate, is not less an insuperable obstacle to a uniformity of interests. The protection of these faculties is the first object of government."

"The executive has no right, in any case, to decide the question, whether there is or is not cause for declaring war."

"Where an excess of power prevails, property of no sort is duly respected. No man is safe in his opinions, his person, his faculties, or his possessions."

"The internal effects of a mutable policy poisons the blessings of liberty itself."

"The operations of the federal government will be most extensive and important in times of war and danger; those of the state governments, in times of peace and security."

"I have no doubt but that the misery of the lower classes will be found to abate whenever the Government assumes a freer aspect and the laws favor a subdivision of Property."

"War should only be declared by the authority of the people, whose toils and treasures are to support its burdens, instead of the government which is to reap its fruits."

"The means of defense against foreign danger historically have become the instruments of tyranny at home."

"What is government itself but the greatest of all reflections on human nature? If men were angels, no government would be necessary. If angels were to govern men, neither external nor internal controls on government would be necessary."

"The rights of persons, and the rights of property, are the objects, for the protection of which Government was instituted."

"In framing a government which is to be administered by men over men you must first enable the government to control the governed; and in the next place oblige it to control itself."

"It will be of little avail to the people that the laws are made by men of their own choice if the laws be so voluminous that they cannot be read, or so incoherent that they cannot be understood."

"To suppose that any form of government will secure liberty or happiness without any virtue in the people is a chimerical idea."

JOHN ADAMS
October 30, 1735 - July 4, 1826

"The essence of a free government consists in an effectual control of rivalries."

"Fear is the foundation of most governments."

"While all other sciences have advanced, that of government is at a standstill - little better understood, little better practiced now than three or four thousand years ago."

"There is danger from all men. The only maxim of a free government ought to be to trust no man living with power to endanger the public liberty."

"A government of laws, and not of men."

"The happiness of society is the end of government."

BENJAMIN FRANKLIN
January 17, 1706 - April 17, 1790

"A great empire, like a great cake, is most easily diminished at the edges."

"Honesty is the best policy."

"Laws too gentle are seldom obeyed; too severe, seldom executed."

"Never confuse motion with action."

"The strictest law sometimes becomes the severest injustice."

"Half a truth is often a great lie."

MERCY OTIS WARREN
September 25, 1728 - October 19, 1814

"The United States form a young republic, a confederacy which ought ever to be cemented by a union of interests and affection, under the influence of those principles which obtained their independence."

JAMES MONROE
April 28, 1758 - July 4, 1831

"National honor is the national property of the highest value."

"The best form of government is that which is most likely to prevent the greatest sum of evil."

THOMAS JEFFERSON
April 13, 1743 - July 4, 1826

"The natural progress of things is for liberty to yield and government to gain ground."

"That government is the strongest of which every man feels himself a part."

"Every government degenerates when trusted to the rulers of the people alone. The people themselves are its only safe depositories."

"If we can but prevent the government from wasting the labours of the people, under the pretence of taking care of them, they must become happy."

"A wise and frugal government, which shall restrain men from injuring one another, shall leave them otherwise free to regulate their own pursuits of industry and improvement, and shall not take from the mouth of labor the bread it has earned."

"The care of human life and happiness, and not their destruction, is the first and only object of good government."

"Were it left to me to decide whether we should have a government without newspapers, or newspapers without a government, I should not hesitate a moment to prefer the latter."

"History, in general, only informs us of what bad government is."

"A Bill of Rights is what the people are entitled to against every government, and what no just government should refuse, or rest on inference."

"We hold these truths to be self-evident: that all men are created equal; that they are endowed by their Creator with certain unalienable rights; that among these are life, liberty, and the pursuit of happiness."

ABRAHAM LINCOLN
February 12, 1809 - April 15, 1865

"We find ourselves under the government of a system of political institutions, conducing more essentially to the ends of civil and religious liberty, than any of which the history of former times tells us."

"I go for all sharing the privileges of the government, who assist in bearing its burdens. Consequently, I go for admitting all whites to the right of suffrage, who pay taxes or bear arms (by no means excluding females)."

"The people will save their government, if the government itself will allow them."

"The best way to get a bad law repealed is to enforce it strictly.

MARK TWAIN (Samuel Clemens)
November 30, 1835 - April 21, 1910

"Patriotism is supporting your country all the time, and your government when it deserves it."

"There is no distinctly American criminal class - except Congress."

"What is the difference between a taxidermist and a tax collector? The taxidermist takes only your skin."

THEODORE 'TEDDY' ROOSEVELT
October 27, 1858 - January 6, 1919

"Order without liberty and liberty without order are equally destructive."

"No man is above the law and no man is below it: nor do we ask any man's permission when we ask him to obey it."

"Obedience of the law is demanded; not asked as a favor."

"It is difficult to make our material condition better by the best law, but it is easy enough to ruin it by bad laws."

"Every immigrant who comes here should be required within five years to learn English or leave the country."

"The American people abhor a vacuum."

"Behind the ostensible government sits enthroned an invisible government owing no allegiance and acknowledging no responsibility to the people."

"A man who is good enough to shed his blood for the country is good enough to be given a square deal afterwards."

WILL ROGERS
November 4, 1879 - August 15, 1935

"I bet after seeing us, George Washington would sue us for calling him 'father.'"

"About all I can say for the United States Senate is that it opens with a prayer and closes with an investigation."

"We will never have true civilization until we have learned to recognize the rights of others."

"Our constitution protects aliens, drunks and U.S. Senators."

"If I studied all my life, I couldn't think up half the number of funny things passed in one session of congress."

"There ought to be one day - just one - when there is open season on senators."

"There's no trick to being a humorist when you have the whole government working for you."

"Things in our country run in spite of government, not by aid of it."

"On account of being a democracy and run by the people, we are the only nation in the world that has to keep a government four years, no matter what it does."

"I don't make jokes. I just watch the government and report the facts."

"Be thankful we're not getting all the government we're paying for."

"The only difference between death and taxes is that death doesn't get worse every time Congress meets."

"If you make any money, the government shoves you in the creek once a year with it in your pockets, and all that don't get wet you can keep."

"We don't seem to be able to check crime, so why not legalize it and then tax it out of business?"

"This country has come to feel the same when Congress is in session as when the baby gets hold of a hammer."

"The income tax has made liars out of more Americans than golf."

ALBERT EINSTEIN
March 14, 1879 - April 18, 1955

"The hardest thing to understand in the world is the income tax."

"Never do anything against conscience even if the state demands it."

DOUGLAS MACARTHUR
January 26, 1880 - April 5, 1964

"Always there has been some terrible evil at home or some monstrous foreign power that was going to gobble us up if we did not blindly rally behind it."

"I am concerned for the security of our great Nation; not so much because of any threat from without, but because of the insidious forces working from within."

"Our government has kept us in a perpetual state of fear - kept us in a continuous stampede of patriotic fervor - with the cry of grave national emergency."

"Our country is now geared to an arms economy bred in an artificially induced psychosis of war hysteria and an incessant propaganda of fear."

MILTON FRIEDMAN
July 31, 1912 - November 16, 2006

"I am favor of cutting taxes under any circumstances and for any excuse, for any reason, whenever it's possible."

"Inflation is the one form of taxation that can be imposed without legislation."

"Governments never learn. Only people learn."

"The government solution to a problem is usually as bad as the problem."

"The world runs on individuals pursuing their self interests. The great achievements of civilization have not come from government bureaus. Einstein didn't construct his theory under order from a bureaucrat. Henry Ford didn't revolutionize the automobile industry that way."

"Only government can take perfectly good paper, cover it with perfectly good ink and make the combination worthless."

"Nothing is so permanent as a temporary government program."

"We have a system that increasingly taxes work and subsidizes nonwork."

"The most important ways in which I think the Internet will affect the big issue is that it will make it more difficult for government to collect taxes."

"The greatest advances of civilization, whether in architecture or painting, in science and literature, in industry or agriculture, have never come from centralized government."

"Many people want the government to protect the consumer. A much more urgent problem is to protect the consumer from the government."

"If you put the federal government in charge of the Sahara Desert, in 5 years there'd be a shortage of sand."

DWIGHT DAVID 'IKE' EISENHOWER
October 14, 1890 - March 28, 1969

"There are a number of things wrong with Washington. One of them is that everyone is too far from home."

"I think that people want peace so much that one of these days government had better get out of their way and let them have it."

"A people that values its privileges above its principles soon loses both."

"How far you can go without destroying from within what you are trying to defend from without?"

ROBERT HEINLEIN
July 7, 1907 - May 8, 1988

"When any government, or any church for that matter, undertakes to say to its subjects, This you may not read, this you must not see, this you are forbidden to know, the end result is tyranny and oppression no matter how holy the motives."

"No statement should be believed because it is made by an authority."

"Be wary of strong drink. It can make you shoot at tax collectors... and miss."

"A society that gets rid of all its troublemakers goes downhill."

"Being right too soon is socially unacceptable."

"Never underestimate the power of human stupidity."

EDWARD TELLER
January 15, 1908 - September 9, 2003

"Secrecy, once accepted, becomes an addiction."

RONALD REAGAN
February 6, 1911 - June 5, 2004

"Government does not solve problems; it subsidizes them."

"Protecting the rights of even the least individual among us is basically the only excuse the government has for even existing."

"No government ever voluntarily reduces itself in size. Government programs, once launched, never disappear. Actually, a government bureau is the nearest thing to eternal life we'll ever see on this earth!"

"Government is like a baby. An alimentary canal with a big appetite at one end and no sense of responsibility at the other."

"Government's first duty is to protect the people, not run their lives."

"Man is not free unless government is limited."

"Governments tend not to solve problems, only to rearrange them."

"Welfare's purpose should be to eliminate, as far as possible, the need for its own existence."

"We should measure welfare's success by how many people leave welfare, not by how many are added."

"Today, if you invent a better mousetrap, the government comes along with a better mouse."

"The best minds are not in government. If any were, business would steal them away."

"One way to make sure crime doesn't pay would be to let the government run it."

"We might come closer to balancing the budget if all of us lived closer to the Commandments and the Golden Rule."

"Government always finds a need for whatever money it gets."

"The problem is not that people are taxed too little, the problem is that government spends too much."

"The most terrifying words in the English language are: I'm from the government and I'm here to help."

"We have the duty to protect the life of an unborn child."

"Government exists to protect us from each other. Where government has gone beyond its limits is in deciding to protect us from ourselves."

"We must reject the idea that every time a law's broken, society is guilty rather than the lawbreaker. It is time to restore the American precept that each individual is accountable for his actions."

"Government's view of the economy could be summed up in a few short phrases: If it moves, tax it. If it keeps moving, regulate it. And if it stops moving, subsidize it."

"I have wondered at times what the Ten Commandments would have looked like if Moses had run them through the US Congress."

RICHARD NIXON
January 9, 1913 - April 22, 1994

"We must always remember that America is a great nation today not because of what the government did for people but because of what people did for themselves and for one another."

"At home, we must reject the mistaken notion - a notion that has dominated too much of the public dialogue for too long - that ever bigger government is the answer to every problem."

"We are not spending the Federal government's money, we are spending the taxpayer's money, and it must be spent in a way which guarantees his money's worth and yields the fullest possible benefit to the people being helped."

"Black Americans, no more than white Americans, they do not want more government programs which perpetuate dependency. They don't want to be a colony in a nation."

"If we take the route of the permanent handout, the American character will itself be impoverished."

"Sure there are dishonest men in local government. But there are dishonest men in national government too."

"The answer to many of the domestic problems we face is not higher taxes and more spending. It is less waste, more results and greater freedom for the individual American to earn a rightful place in his own community - and for States and localities to address their own needs in their own ways, in the light of their own priorities."

JOHN FITZGERALD KENNEDY
May 29, 1917 - November 22, 1963

"A nation which has forgotten the quality of courage which in the past has been brought to public life is not as likely to insist upon or regard that quality in its chosen leaders today - and in fact we have forgotten."

"My fellow Americans, ask not what your country can do for you, ask what you can do for your country."

"I look forward to a great future for America - a future in which our country will match its military strength with our moral restraint, its wealth with our wisdom, its power with our purpose."

BILLY GRAHAM
November 7, 1918

"I believe the home and marriage is the foundation of our society and must be protected."

"Regardless of what society says, we can't go on much longer in the sea of immorality without judgment coming."

"Our society strives to avoid any possibility of offending anyone - except God."

"Old is authentic. Old is genuine. Old is valuable."

"Self-centered indulgence, pride and a lack of shame over sin are now emblems of the American lifestyle."

"The framers of our Constitution meant we were to have freedom of religion, not freedom from religion."

ROBERT KENNEDY
November 20, 1925 - June 6, 1968

"Every society gets the kind of criminal it deserves. What is equally true is that every community gets the kind of law enforcement it insists on."

"Whenever men take the law into their own hands, the loser is the law. And when the law loses, freedom languishes."

MARTIN LUTHER KING JR.
January 15, 1929 - April 4, 1968

"A nation or civilization that continues to produce soft-minded men purchases its own spiritual death on the installment plan."

"I have a dream that my four little children will one day live in a nation where they will not be judged by the color of their skin, but by the content of their character."

"We must learn to live together as brothers or perish together as fools."

"I have a dream that one day every valley shall be exalted, every hill and mountain shall be made low, the rough places will be made straight and the glory of the Lord shall be revealed and all flesh shall see it together."

"I look to a day when people will not be judged by the color of their skin, but by the content of their character."

"Injustice anywhere is a threat to justice everywhere."

RON PAUL
August 20, 1935

"When the federal government spends more each year than it collects in tax revenues, it has three choices: It can raise taxes, print money, or borrow money. While these actions may benefit politicians, all three options are bad for average Americans."

"Why is it claimed that if people won't or can't take care of their own needs, that people in government can do it for them?"

"When one gets in bed with government, one must expect the diseases it spreads."

"I am absolutely opposed to a national ID card. This is a total contradiction of what a free society is all about. The purpose of government is to protect the secrecy and the privacy of all individuals, not the secrecy of government. We don't need a national ID card."

"1913 wasn't a very good year. 1913 gave us the income tax, the 16th amendment and the IRS."

"Having federal officials, whether judges, bureaucrats, or congressmen, impose a new definition of marriage on the people is an act of social engineering profoundly hostile to liberty."

"The obligations of our representatives in Washington are to protect our liberty, not coddle the world, precipitating no-win wars, while bringing bankruptcy and economic turmoil to our people."

"There is nothing wrong with describing Conservatism as protecting the Constitution, protecting all things that limit government. Government is the enemy of liberty. Government should be very restrained."

GEORGE CARLIN
May 12, 1937 - June 22, 2008

"If we could just find out who's in charge, we could kill him."

BEN CARSON
September 18, 1951

"What I agree with is that we need a significantly changed taxation system. And the one that I've advocated is based on tithing, because I think God is a pretty fair guy. And he said, you know, if you give me a tithe, it doesn't matter how much you make."

"Our strength as a nation comes in our unity. We are the United States of America, not the divided states. And those who want to divide us are trying to divide us, and we shouldn't let them do it."

"We have the purveyors of hatred who take every single incident between people of two races and try to make a race war out of it and drive wedges into people. And this does not need to be done."

"There is so much potential out there in young people and they aren't getting the right information or being encouraged in the right ways. This is our duty as a society."

"I want the government to provide the military so we don't get invaded by somebody and destroyed. I want the government to provide the roads so I can get from point A to B. In terms of taking care of my day to day needs, I want to do that myself. I want my community to do that."

"The fact that our government is using instruments of government like the IRS to punish its opponents; this is not the kind of thing that is a Democrat or a Republican issue. This is an American issue... A lot of people do not feel free to express themselves."

DENNIS MILLER
November 3, 1953

"Washington, DC is to lying what Wisconsin is to cheese."

"Elected office holds more perks than Elvis' nightstand."

RAND PAUL
January 7, 1963

"I don't want to live in a nanny state where people are telling me where I can go and what I can do."

"For too long, we've attached some mythic notion to government solutions, and yet, 40 years after we began the War on Poverty, poverty still abounds."

"I don't want my marriage or my guns registered in Washington. And if people have an opinion, it's a religious opinion that is heartily felt, obviously they should be allowed to practice that and no government should interfere with them."

"I would argue that the objective evidence shows that big government is not a friend to African Americans."

"The history of African-American repression in this country rose from government-sanctioned racism. Jim Crow laws were a product of bigoted state and local governments."

"The government has a history of not treating people fairly, from the internment of Japanese Americans in World War II to African-Americans in the Civil Rights era."

"Government can supply bread, but it can't mend a broken spirit."

"A free society will abide unofficial, private discrimination, even when that means allowing hate-filled groups to exclude people based on the color of their skin."

"Really, having a gun registry and having to rely on the government to keep it secret, the government isn't so great at keeping confidences."

"Laws don't really restrain people. Ninety-eight percent of people follow a virtuous course with or without laws."

"We live in a democracy, and people are free to sometimes choose the wrong leader."

"In a free society, we will tolerate boorish people, who have abhorrent behavior, but as civilized people, we publicly criticize that, and don't belong to those groups or don't associate with those people."

"Big and oppressive government has long been the enemy of freedom, something black Americans know all too well."

"I don't care if you're a Republican or a Democrat; there is something profoundly un-American about using the brute force of government to bully someone."

"We don't need bigger government. We need to shrink the size of government."

"All issues of crime are better addressed at the state level."

"I, for one, will remain constantly vigilant of a government that admits its transgressions of liberty only when they are caught lying."
"
"When the government tries to invade the church to enforce its own opinion on marriage, that's when it's time to resist."

"Marriage has always been a state and local issue."

"America is a world leader, but we should not be its policeman or ATM."

"The state doesn't own your children. Parents own the children."

"Just because a majority of the Supreme Court declares something to be 'constitutional' does not make it so."

TED CRUZ
December 22, 1970

"When, President Obama, do you mean to cease abusing our patience? How long is that madness of yours still to mock us? When is there to be an end to that unbridled audacity of yours swaggering about as it does now?"

"The American president has a peculiar leadership responsibility to speak out for freedom."

"We need a president who is willing to uphold the law."

"We need to make clear the federal government does not have authority to indefinitely detain U.S. citizens without due process or, for that matter, to use lethal force on U.S. citizens on U.S. soil if they don't pose imminent threats."

"Every American, I think, should be able to fill out their taxes on a postcard."

"When you tell the American people, 'Read my lips. No new taxes,' that should mean no new taxes."

"Washington has, with some justification, gained a reputation for being hopelessly mired in partisan gridlock."

"No major entitlement, once it has been implemented, has ever been unwound."

"It is very true that D.C. often operates in the land of caricature."

"One of the specific powers and responsibilities of the federal government is to secure the borders."

"I've spent the past month in Washington, D.C., and it is terrific to be back in America."

"You want to know what judicial activism is? Judicial activism is judges imposing their policy preferences on the words of the Constitution."

"I don't think the federal government has any business keeping a list of law-abiding Americans who exercise their constitutional right to keep and bear arms."

"When you subpoena one pastor, you subpoena every pastor."

THOMAS SOWELL
June 30, 1930

"Being willing to donate the taxpayers' money is not the same as being willing to put your own money where your mouth is."

"It is a way to take people's wealth from them without having to openly raise taxes. Inflation is the most universal tax of all."

"Those who cry out that the government should 'do something' never even ask for data on what has actually happened when the government did something, compared to what actually happened when the government did nothing."

"The Congressional Budget Office has been embarrassed repeatedly by making projections based on the assumption that tax revenues and tax rates move in the same direction."

"The real goal should be reduced government spending, rather than balanced budgets achieved by ever rising tax rates to cover ever rising spending."

"What 'multiculturalism' boils down to is that you can praise any culture in the world except Western culture - and you cannot blame any culture in the world except Western culture."

"Life in general has never been even close to fair, so the pretense that the government can make it fair is a valuable and inexhaustible asset to politicians who want to expand government."

"The more people who are dependent on government handouts, the more votes the left can depend on for an ever-expanding welfare state."

"You will never understand bureaucracies until you understand that for bureaucrats procedure is everything and outcomes are nothing."

"What is ominous is the ease with which some people go from saying that they don't like something to saying that the government should forbid it. When you go down that road, don't expect freedom to survive very long."

"The welfare state is not really about the welfare of the masses. It is about the egos of the elites."

CLINT EASTWOOD
May 31, 1930

"Society is at odds with itself."

"I'm not a reality-TV kind of guy. But it's almost like we're living in a reality show. Every day in this country, everybody keeps worrying about the deterioration of America, and it's like a big reality show."

"Some people feel that the world owes them a living."

CHUCK NORRIS
March 10, 1940

"Unfortunately, people are re-interpreting the Constitution as a living document, and it's not. It's a solid-based document and it shouldn't be played with."

III
ON RELIGION, MORALITY & PROVERBS

"It is impossible to reason without arriving at a Supreme Being."- George Washington

BENJAMIN FRANKLIN
January 17, 1706 - April 17, 1790

"How few there are who have courage enough to own their faults, or resolution enough to mend them."

"The doorstep to the temple of wisdom is a knowledge of our own ignorance."

"As we must account for every idle word, so must we account for every idle silence."

"Wise men don't need advice. Fools won't take it."

"It takes many good deeds to build a good reputation, and only one bad one to lose it."

"Be at war with your vices, at peace with your neighbors, and let every new year find you a better man."

"Content makes poor men rich; discontent makes rich men poor."

"Well done is better than well said."

"Who had deceived thee so often as thyself?"

"Early to bed and early to rise makes a man healthy, wealthy and wise."

"In the affairs of this world, men are saved not by faith, but by the want of it."

"Many foxes grow gray but few grow good."

"Do not fear mistakes. You will know failure. Continue to reach out."

"Honesty is the best policy."

"There are three things extremely hard: steel, a diamond, and to know one's self."

"Those that won't be counseled can't be helped."

"In reality, there is, perhaps, no one of our natural passions so hard to subdue as pride."

"A false friend and a shadow attend only while the sun shines."

"Work as if you were to live a hundred years. Pray as if you were to die tomorrow."

"Trouble springs from idleness, and grievous toil from needless ease."

"Observe all men, thyself most."

"He that sows thorns should never go barefoot."

"Where sense is wanting, everything is wanting."

"Speak ill of no man, but speak all the good you know of everybody."

"Words may show a man's wit but actions his meaning."

"Half a truth is often a great lie."

"If passion drives you, let reason hold the reins."

"Tricks and treachery are the practice of fools, that don't have brains enough to be honest."

"When you're finished changing, you're finished."

"Blessed is he that expects nothing, for he shall never be disappointed."

PATRICK HENRY
May 29, 1736 - June 6, 1799

"The Bible is worth all the other books which have ever been printed."

"This is all the inheritance I give to my dear family. The religion of Christ will give them one which will make them rich indeed

GEORGE WASHINGTON
February 22, 1732 - December 14, 1799

"I am persuaded, you will permit me to observe, that the path of true piety is so plain as to require but little political direction."

"Being no bigot myself to any mode of worship, I am disposed to indulge the professors of Christianity in the church, that road to heaven which to them shall seem the most direct plainest easiest and least liable to exception."

"I beg you be persuaded that no one would be more zealous than myself to establish effectual barriers against the horrors of spiritual tyranny, and every species of religious persecution."

It is impossible to reason without arriving at a Supreme Being."

"It is far better to be alone, than to be in bad company."

"Let us with caution indulge the supposition that morality can be maintained without religion. Reason and experience both forbid us to expect that national morality can prevail in exclusion of religious principle."

"Religion is as necessary to reason as reason is to religion. The one cannot exist without the other. A reasoning being would lose his reason, in attempting to account for the great phenomena of nature, had he not a Supreme Being to refer to; and well has it been said, that if there had been no God, mankind would have been obliged to imagine one."

"The foolish and wicked practice of profane cursing and swearing is a vice so mean and low that every person of sense and character detests and despises it."

"Let your heart feel for the afflictions and distress of everyone, and let your hand give in proportion to your purse."

"Happiness and moral duty are inseparably connected."

"We should not look back unless it is to derive useful lessons from past errors, and for the purpose of profiting by dearly bought experience."

"Labor to keep alive in your breast that little spark of celestial fire, called conscience."

"Associate with men of good quality if you esteem your own reputation; for it is better to be alone than in bad company."

"Let us raise a standard to which the wise and honest can repair; the rest is in the hands of God."

"I hope I shall possess firmness and virtue enough to maintain what I consider the most enviable of all titles, the character of an honest man."

"Truth will ultimately prevail where there is pains to bring it to light."

"Few men have virtue to withstand the highest bidder."

ABIGAIL ADAMS
November 22, 1744 - October 28, 1818

"If we do not lay out ourselves in the service of mankind whom should we serve?"

NATHAN HALE
June 6, 1755 - September 22, 1776

"Shun all vice, especially card playing."

"I wish to be useful, and every kind of service necessary to the public good becomes honorable by being necessary."

NOAH WEBSTER
October 16, 1758 - May 28, 1843

"All the miseries and evils which men suffer from vice, crime, ambition, injustice, oppression, slavery and war, proceed from their despising or neglecting the precepts contained in the Bible."

"The Bible must be considered as the great source of all the truth by which men are to be guided in government as well as in all social transactions."

ALEXANDER HAMILTON
January 11, 1755 - July 12, 1804

"The voice of the people has been said to be the voice of God; and, however generally this maxim has been quoted and believed, it is not true to fact. The people are turbulent and changing, they seldom judge or determine right."

"When the sword is once drawn, the passions of men observe no bounds of moderation."

"The sacred rights of mankind are not to be rummaged for among old parchments or musty records. They are written, as with a sunbeam, in the whole volume of human nature, by the hand of the divinity itself; and can never be erased or obscured by mortal power."

"Those who stand for nothing fall for anything."

"Real firmness is good for anything; strut is good for nothing."

THOMAS PAINE
NE February 9, 1737 - June 8, 1809

"When we are planning for posterity, we ought to remember that virtue is not hereditary."

"Character is much easier kept than recovered."

"An army of principles can penetrate where an army of soldiers cannot."

"Reputation is what men and women think of us; character is what God and angels know of us."

"Moderation in temper is always a virtue; but moderation in principle is always a vice."

"What we obtain too cheap, we esteem too lightly; it is dearness only that gives everything its value."

"I love the man that can smile in trouble, that can gather strength from distress, and grow brave by reflection.'Tis the business of little minds to shrink, but he whose heart is firm, and whose conscience approves his conduct, will pursue his principles unto death."

JOHN PAUL JONES
July 6, 1747 - July 18, 1792

"If fear is cultivated it will become stronger, if faith is cultivated it will achieve mastery."

SAMUEL ADAMS
September 27, 1722 - October 2, 1803

"He who is void of virtuous attachments in private life is, or very soon will be, void of all regard for his country. There is seldom an instance of a man guilty of betraying his country, who had not before lost the feeling of moral obligations in his private connections."

JAMES MADISON
March 16, 1751 - June 28, 1836

"Union of religious sentiments begets a surprising confidence."

JOHN ADAMS
October 30, 1735 - July 4, 1826

"Because power corrupts, society's demands for moral authority and character increase as the importance of the position increases."

"Our Constitution was made only for a moral and religious people. It is wholly inadequate to the government of any other."

"Power always thinks... that it is doing God's service when it is violating all His laws."

"The Hebrews have done more to civilize men than any other nation. If I were an atheist, and believed blind eternal fate, I should still believe that fate had ordained the Jews to be the most essential instrument for civilizing the nations."

THOMAS JEFFERSON
April 13, 1743 - July 4, 1826

"An injured friend is the bitterest of foes."

"Truth is certainly a branch of morality and a very important one to society."

"How much pain they have cost us, the evils which have never happened."

"Power is not alluring to pure minds."

"It takes time to persuade men to do even what is for their own good."

"Be polite to all, but intimate with few."

"Errors of opinion may be tolerated where reason is left free to combat it."

"Ignorance is preferable to error, and he is less remote from the truth who believes nothing than he who believes what is wrong."

"Whenever you do a thing, act as if all the world were watching."

"Wisdom I know is social. She seeks her fellows. But Beauty is jealous, and illy bears the presence of a rival."

"I hope our wisdom will grow with our power, and teach us, that the less we use our power the greater it will be."

"It is in our lives and not our words that our religion must be read."

"I have sworn upon the altar of God, eternal hostility against every form of tyranny over the mind of man."

"Nothing can stop the man with the right mental attitude from achieving his goal; nothing on earth can help the man with the wrong mental attitude."

"Honesty is the first chapter in the book of wisdom."

"One man with courage is a majority."

"I tremble for my country when I reflect that God is just; that his justice cannot sleep forever."

"The God, who gave us life, gave us liberty at the same time."

"When a man assumes a public trust he should consider himself a public property."

ABRAHAM LINCOLN
February 12, 1809 - April 15, 1865

"That I am not a member of any Christian church is true; but I have never denied the truth of the Scriptures, and I have never spoken with intentional disrespect of religion in general, or of any denomination of Christians in particular."

"I go to assume a task more difficult than that which devolved upon Washington. Unless the great God, who assisted him, shall be with me and aid me, I must fail; but if the same omniscient Mind and Almighty arm that directed and protected him shall guide and support me, I shall not fail - I shall succeed."

"In the end, it's not the years in your life that count. It's the life in your years."

"I do not think I could myself be brought to support a man for office whom I knew to be an open enemy of, and scoffer at, religion."

"I know that the Lord is always on the side of the right; but it is my constant anxiety and prayer that I and this nation may be on the Lord's side."

"No policy that does not rest upon some philosophical public opinion can be permanently maintained."

"Important principles may, and must, be inflexible."

"Nearly all men can stand adversity, but if you want to test a man's character, give him power."

"In great contests each party claims to act in accordance with the will of God. Both may be, and one must be wrong."

"Surely God would not have created such a being as man, with an ability to grasp the infinite, to exist only for a day! No, no, man was made for immortality."

"Character is like a tree and reputation like a shadow. The shadow is what we think of it; the tree is the real thing."

"You can fool all the people some of the time, and some of the people all the time, but you cannot fool all the people all the time."

"A house divided against itself cannot stand."

ROBERT EDWARD LEE
January 19, 1807 - October 12, 1870

"In all my perplexities and distresses, the Bible has never failed to give me light and strength."

"My chief concern is to try to be a humble, earnest Christian."

"The trite saying that honesty is the best policy has met with the just criticism that honesty is not policy. The real honest man is honest from conviction of what is right, not from policy."

"Never do a wrong thing to make a friend or to keep one."

"Get correct views of life, and learn to see the world in its true light. It will enable you to live pleasantly, to do good, and, when summoned away, to leave without regret."

"I cannot trust a man to control others who cannot control himself."

"Obedience to lawful authority is the foundation of manly character."

HARRIET TUBMAN
c. March 1822 - March 10, 1913

"Every great dream begins with a dreamer. Always remember, you have within you the strength, the patience, and the passion to reach for the stars to change the world."

"Lord, I'm going to hold steady on to You and You've got to see me through."

MARK TWAIN (Samuel Clemens)
November 30, 1835 - April 21, 1910

"The secret of getting ahead is getting started."

"Kindness is the language which the deaf can hear and the blind can see."

"All you need in this life is ignorance and confidence, and then success is sure."

"We are all alike, on the inside."

"A man cannot be comfortable without his own approval."

"Familiarity breeds contempt - and children."

"Man is the only animal that blushes - or needs to."

"Few things are harder to put up with than the annoyance of a good example."

"By trying we can easily learn to endure adversity. Another man's, I mean."

"Age is an issue of mind over matter. If you don't mind, it doesn't matter."

"There is no sadder sight than a young pessimist."

"If you tell the truth, you don't have to remember anything."

"Don't go around saying the world owes you a living. The world owes you nothing. It was here first."

"When in doubt tell the truth."

"Do the thing you fear most and the death of fear is certain."

"Golf is a good walk spoiled."

"All generalizations are false, including this one."

"It is better to deserve honors and not have them than to have them and not deserve them."

"Courage is resistance to fear, mastery of fear, not absence of fear."

"The first of April is the day we remember what we are the other 364 days of the year."

"Let us endeavor so to live so that when we come to die even the undertaker will be sorry."

"If man could be crossed with the cat it would improve man, but deteriorate the cat."

"Man will do many things to get himself loved; he will do all things to get himself envied."

"I am an old man and have known a great many troubles, but most of them never happened."

"Thousands of geniuses live and die undiscovered - either by themselves or by others."

DWIGHT LYMAN MOODY
February 5, 1837 - December 22, 1899

"Faith makes all things possible... love makes all things easy."

"The Bible will keep you from sin, or sin will keep you from the Bible."

"We can stand affliction better than we can prosperity, for in prosperity we forget God."

"There are many of us that are willing to do great things for the Lord, but few of us are willing to do little things."

"Where I was born and where and how I have lived is unimportant. It is what I have done with where I have been that should be of interest."

"Character is what a man is in the dark."

"If I take care of my character, my reputation will take care of me."

"I have had more trouble with myself than with any other man."

"There's no better book with which to defend the Bible than the Bible itself."

"No man can resolve himself into Heaven."

"A good example is far better than a good precept."

THEODORE 'TEDDY' ROOSEVELT
October 27, 1858 - January 6, 1919

"No man is justified in doing evil on the ground of expedience."

"The only man who never makes a mistake is the man who never does anything."

"Nobody cares how much you know, until they know how much you care."

"A thorough knowledge of the Bible is worth more than a college education."

WILL ROGERS
November 4, 1879 - August 15, 1935

"Don't let yesterday use up too much of today."

"The best way out of a difficulty is through it."

"What the country needs is dirtier fingernails and cleaner minds."

"Lettin' the cat outta the bag is a whole lot easier 'n puttin' it back in."

"Good judgment comes from experience, and a lot of that comes from bad judgment."

"Even if you're on the right track, you'll get run over if you just sit there."

"You've got to go out on a limb sometimes because that's where the fruit is."

"Too many people spend money they haven't earned to buy things they don't want to impress people they don't like."

GEORGE WASHINGTON CARVER
c. 1860 - January 5, 1943

"I love to think of nature as an unlimited broadcasting station, through which God speaks to us every hour, if we will only tune in."

"Where there is no vision, there is no hope."

"Nothing is more beautiful than the loveliness of the woods before sunrise."

THOMAS EDISON
February 11, 1847 - October 18, 1931

"I know this world is ruled by infinite intelligence. Everything that surrounds us- everything that exists - proves that there are infinite laws behind it. There can be no denying this fact. It is mathematical in its precision."

HENRY FORD
July 30, 1863 - April 7, 1947

"I believe God is managing affairs and that He doesn't need any advice from me. With God in charge, I believe everything will work out for the best in the end. So what is there to worry about?"

"Anyone who stops learning is old, whether at twenty or eighty. Anyone who keeps learning stays young. The greatest thing in life is to keep your mind young."

ALBERT EINSTEIN
March 14, 1879 - April 18, 1955

"I shall never believe that God plays dice with the world."

"God always takes the simplest way."

"Science without religion is lame, religion without science is blind."

"The world is a dangerous place to live; not because of the people who are evil, but because of the people who don't do anything about it."

"Most people say that it is the intellect which makes a great scientist. They are wrong: it is character."

"Weakness of attitude becomes weakness of character."

DOUGLAS MACARTHUR
January 26, 1880 - April 5, 1964

"Build me a son, O Lord, who will be strong enough to know when he is weak, and brave enough to face himself when he is afraid, one who will be proud and unbending in honest defeat, and humble and gentle in victory."

"A better world shall emerge based on faith and understanding."

"Age wrinkles the body. Quitting wrinkles the soul."

GEORGE CATLETT MARSHALL
December 31, 1880 - October 16, 1959

"Don't fight the problem, decide it."

HELEN KELLER
June 27, 1880 - June 1, 1968

"Unless we form the habit of going to the Bible in bright moments as well as in trouble, we cannot fully respond to its consolations because we lack equilibrium between light and darkness."

"I can see, and that is why I can be happy, in what you call the dark, but which to me is golden. I can see a God-made world, not a manmade world."

"It is wonderful how much time good people spend fighting the devil. If they would only expend the same amount of energy loving their fellow men, the devil would die in his own tracks of ennui."

"It is for us to pray not for tasks equal to our powers, but for powers equal to our tasks, to go forward with a great desire forever beating at the door of our hearts as we travel toward our distant goal."

"Faith is the strength by which a shattered world shall emerge into the light."

"The best and most beautiful things in the world cannot be seen or even touched - they must be felt with the heart."

"Walking with a friend in the dark is better than walking alone in the light."

"Everything has its wonders, even darkness and silence, and I learn whatever state I may be in, therein to be content."

"Once I knew only darkness and stillness... my life was without past or future... but a little word from the fingers of another fell into my hand that clutched at emptiness and my heart leaped to the rapture of living."

"Death is no more than passing from one room into another. But there's a difference for me, you know. Because in that other room I shall be able to see."

"It is a terrible thing to see and have no vision."

"When we do the best that we can, we never know what miracle is wrought in our life, or in the life of another."

"No one has a right to consume happiness without producing it."

JULIAN HENRY 'GROUCHO' MARX
October 2, 1890 - August 19, 1977

"The secret of life is honesty and fair dealing. If you can fake that, you've got it made."

JULIUS ROBERT OPPENHEIMER
April 22, 1904 - February 18, 1967

"In some sort of crude sense, which no vulgarity, no humor, no overstatement can quite extinguish, the physicists have known sin; and this is a knowledge which they cannot lose."

ROBERT HEINLEIN
July 7, 1907 - May 8, 1988

"To be matter-of-fact about the world is to blunder into fantasy - and dull fantasy at that, as the real world is strange and wonderful."

"One of the sanest, surest, and most generous joys of life comes from being happy over the good fortune of others."

JOHN ARCHIBALD WHEELER
July 9, 1911 - April 13, 2008

"If you haven't found something strange during the day, it hasn't been much of a day."

RONALD REAGAN
February 6, 1911 - June 5, 2004

"Without God, democracy will not and cannot long endure."

"Within the covers of the Bible are the answers for all the problems men face."

"We are never defeated unless we give up on God."

"Freedom prospers when religion is vibrant and the rule of law under God is acknowledged."

"There are no easy answers, but there are simple answers. We must have the courage to do what we know is morally right."

"We have the duty to protect the life of an unborn child."

"If we ever forget that we are One Nation Under God, then we will be a nation gone under."

"There are no constraints on the human mind, no walls around the human spirit, no barriers to our progress except those we ourselves erect."

"We can't help everyone, but everyone can help someone."

"There are no great limits to growth because there are no limits of human intelligence, imagination, and wonder."

RICHARD NIXON
January 9, 1913 - April 22, 1994

"My concern today is not with the length of a person's hair but with his conduct."

"The finest steel has to go through the hottest fire."

JOHN FITZGERALD KENNEDY
May 29, 1917 - November 22, 1963

"A man may die, nations may rise and fall, but an idea lives on."

BILLY GRAHAM
November 7, 1918

"Man is not born to atheism. He is born to believe."

"I've read the last page of the Bible. It's all going to turn out all right."

"'Suffering should not make us bitter people,' my mother once said, 'it should make us better comforters.' Young people need to hear this from those who have walked before them, because someday they'll be walking those same steps, but there may not be anyone following behind."

"I think it is a sin to look at another person as inferior to yourself because of race or because of ethnic background, and I think the greatest thing to do is to pray that God will give you love for them, and I do."

"The thing that alarms me is that there are so many clergymen who say that the so-called 'new morality' is all right. They say we're living in a new generation; let's be relevant, let's change God's law. Let's say that adultery is all right under certain circumstances; fornication's all right under certain circumstances. If it's 'meaningful...'"

"God is more interested in your future and your relationships than you are."

"The human heart is the same the world over."

"We're all sinners. Everybody you meet all over the world is a sinner."

"Man has two great spiritual needs. One is for forgiveness. The other is for goodness."

"No one can outrun death. It will catch up to all of us eventually."

"You're born. You suffer. You die. Fortunately, there's a loophole."

MARTIN LUTHER KING JR.
January 15, 1929 - April 4, 1968

"Science investigates; religion interprets. Science gives man knowledge which is power; religion gives man wisdom which is control."

"Faith is taking the step even when you don't see the whole staircase."

"Our scientific power has outrun our spiritual power. We have guided missiles and misguided men."

"The time is always right to do what is right."

"Love is the only force capable of transforming an enemy into friend."

GEORGE CARLIN
May 12, 1937 - June 22, 2008

"May the forces of evil become confused on the way to your house."

"Inside every cynical person, there is a disappointed idealist."

STEPHEN CHARLES BLANDINO
November 16, 1941 - June 16, 2006

"I fell out of the Ugly tree and hit every branch on the way down."

ROBERT ZITTEL
November 5, 1948 - November 7, 2013

"Who is your brother's keeper?"

BEN CARSON
September 18, 1951

"Through hard work, perseverance and a faith in God, you can live your dreams."

RAND PAUL
January 7, 1963

"As a Christian, I believe in redemption. And I believe in second chances."

"I believe that in the historic and religious nature, marriage is between a man and a woman."

TED CRUZ
December 22, 1970

"I am blessed to receive a word from God every day in receiving the Scriptures and reading the Scriptures. And God speaks through the Bible."

"The hard-core Left loves ridiculing Christians who believe scripture that says, 'God created the heaven and the earth.' They say that it's anti-science to believe that an almighty God would do such a thing."

"If you hate the Jewish people, you are not reflecting the teachings of Christ."

"Those who hate Israel hate America. Those who hate Jews hate Christians."

"If you will not stand with Israel and the Jews, then I will not stand with you."

"Christians have no greater ally than Israel."

THOMAS SOWELL
June 30, 1930

"Without a moral framework, there is nothing left but immediate self-indulgence by some and the path of least resistance by others. Neither can sustain a free society."

CLINT EASTWOOD
May 31, 1930

"Respect your efforts, respect yourself. Self-respect leads to self-discipline. When you have both firmly under your belt, that's real power."

Sometimes if you want to see a change for the better, you have to take things into your own hands.

"If you want a guarantee, buy a toaster."

"If you think it's going to rain, it will."

JOHN WAYNE
May 26, 1907 - June 11, 1979

"Courage is being scared to death... and saddling up anyway."

"Tomorrow hopes we have learned something from yesterday."

CHUCK NORRIS
March 10, 1940

"Men are like steel. When they lose their temper, they lose their worth."

"It's amazing because people come up to me and say, 'Chuck, you're the luckiest guy in the world to be a world karate champion and a movie and TV star.' When they say this to me, I kind of smile because luck had nothing to do with it; God had everything to do with it."

"Good morals lead to good laws."

GEORGE EASTMAN
July 12, 1854 - March 14, 1932

"What we do during our working hours determines what we have; what we do in our leisure hours determines what we are."

RICHARD BUCKMINSTER 'BUCKY' FULLER
July 12, 1895 - July 1, 1983

"There is nothing in a caterpillar that tells you it's going to be a butterfly."

"A proverb is much matter distilled into few words."

IV
ON WAR, CONFLICT & PEACE

"The soldier above all others prays for peace, for it is the soldier who must suffer and bear the deepest wounds and scars of war." - Douglas MacArthur

JAMES MADISON
March 16, 1751 - June 28, 1836

"Each generation should be made to bear the burden of its own wars, instead of carrying them on, at the expense of other generations."

BENJAMIN FRANKLIN
January 17, 1706 - April 17, 1790

"When will mankind be convinced and agree to settle their difficulties by arbitration?"

"All wars are follies, very expensive and very mischievous ones."

"Wars are not paid for in wartime, the bill comes later."

"There was never a good war, or a bad peace."

"Even peace may be purchased at too high a price."

MERCY OTIS WARREN
September 25, 1728 - October 19, 1814

"The bulk of mankind have indeed, in all countries in their turn, been made the prey of ambition."

THOMAS PAINE
February 9, 1737 - June 8, 1809

"He who is the author of a war lets loose the whole contagion of hell and opens a vein that bleeds a nation to death."

JAMES MONROE
April 28, 1758 - July 4, 1831

"Preparation for war is a constant stimulus to suspicion and ill will."

THOMAS JEFFERSON
April 13, 1743 - July 4, 1826

"I abhor war and view it as the greatest scourge of mankind."

"War is an instrument entirely inefficient toward redressing wrong; and multiplies, instead of indemnifying losses."

"The most successful war seldom pays for its losses."

"I have seen enough of one war never to wish to see another."

"It is incumbent on every generation to pay its own debts as it goes. A principle which if acted on would save one-half the wars of the world."

"It is our duty still to endeavor to avoid war; but if it shall actually take place, no matter by whom brought on, we must defend ourselves. If our house be on fire, without inquiring whether it was fired from within or without, we must try to extinguish it."

"We did not raise armies for glory or for conquest."

GEORGE WASHINGTON
February 22, 1732 - December 14, 1799

"War - An act of violence whose object is to constrain the enemy, to accomplish our will."

"To be prepared for war is one of the most effective means of preserving peace."

ABRAHAM LINCOLN
February 12, 1809 - April 15, 1865

"Allow the president to invade a neighboring nation whenever he shall deem it necessary to repel an invasion and you allow him to do so whenever he may choose to say he deems it necessary for such purpose - and you allow him to make war at pleasure."

WILLIAM SHERMAN
February 8, 1820 - February 14, 1891

"War is cruelty. There is no use trying to reform it. The crueler it is, the sooner it will be over."

"I am tired and sick of war. Its glory is all moonshine. It is only those who have neither fired a shot nor heard the shrieks and groans of the wounded who cry aloud for blood, for vengeance, for desolation. War is hell."

"The scenes on this field would have cured anybody of war."

"War is the remedy that our enemies have chosen, and I say let us give them all they want."

"In our Country... one class of men makes war and leaves another to fight it out."

"I think I understand what military fame is; to be killed on the field of battle and have your name misspelled in the newspapers."

"I know I had no hand in making this war, and I know I will make more sacrifices today than any of you to secure peace."

"There's many a boy here today who looks on war as all glory but it is all hell."

"War is at its best, barbarism."

ROBERT EDWARD LEE
January 19, 1807 - October 12, 1870

"It is good that war is so horrible, or we might grow to like it."

"What a cruel thing war is... to fill our hearts with hatred instead of love for our neighbors."

"The war... was an unnecessary condition of affairs, and might have been avoided if forbearance and wisdom had been practiced on both sides."

"It is well that war is so terrible, otherwise we should grow too fond of it."

"I have been up to see the Congress and they do not seem to be able to do anything except to eat peanuts and chew tobacco, while my army is starving."

THEODORE 'TEDDY' ROOSEVELT
October 27, 1858 - January 6, 1919

"Wars are, of course, as a rule to be avoided; but they are far better than certain kinds of peace."

"The pacifist is as surely a traitor to his country and to humanity as is the most brutal wrongdoer."

WILL ROGERS
November 4, 1879 - August 15, 1935

"You can't say civilization don't advance... in every war they kill you in a new way."

"I have a scheme for stopping war. It's this - no nation is allowed to enter a war till they have paid for the last one."

ALBERT EINSTEIN
March 14, 1879 - April 18, 1955

"I know not with what weapons World War III will be fought, but World War IV will be fought with sticks and stones."

"It has become appallingly obvious that our technology has exceeded our humanity."

"Technological progress is like an axe in the hands of a pathological criminal."

"Force always attracts men of low morality."

DOUGLAS MACARTHUR
January 26, 1880 - April 5, 1964

"My first recollection is that of a bugle call."

"I suppose, in a way, this has become part of my soul. It is a symbol of my life. Whatever I have done that really matters, I've done wearing it. When the time comes, it will be in this that I journey forth. What greater honor could come to an American, and a soldier?"

"In my dreams I hear again the crash of guns, the rattle of musketry, the strange, mournful mutter of the battlefield."

"One cannot wage war under present conditions without the support of public opinion, which is tremendously molded by the press and other forms of propaganda."

"Could I have but a line a century hence crediting a contribution to the advance of peace, I would yield every honor which has been accorded by war."

"It is fatal to enter any war without the will to win it."

"In war, you win or lose, live or die - and the difference is just an eyelash."

"They died hard, those savage men - like wounded wolves at bay. They were filthy, and they were lousy, and they stunk. And I loved them."

"The soldier above all others prays for peace, for it is the soldier who must suffer and bear the deepest wounds and scars of war."

"Duty, Honor, Country. Those three hallowed words reverently dictate what you ought to be, what you can be, what you will be."

"Like the old soldier of the ballad, I now close my military career and just fade away, an old soldier who tried to do his duty as God gave him the light to see that duty. Goodbye."

GEORGE CATLETT MARSHALL
December 31, 1880 - October 16, 1959

"I can't expect loyalty from the army if I do not give it."

"The only way human beings can win a war is to prevent it.

"If man does find the solution for world peace it will be the most revolutionary reversal of his record we have ever known."

HELEN KELLER
June 27, 1880 - June 1, 1968

"Strike against war, for without you no battles can be fought!"

"As the eagle was killed by the arrow winged with his own feather, so the hand of the world is wounded by its own skill."

GEORGE SMITH PATTON
November 11, 1885 - December 21, 1945

"The object of war is not to die for your country but to make the other bastard die for his."

"Americans love to fight. All real Americans love the sting of battle."

"A pint of sweat saves a gallon of blood."

"We herd sheep, we drive cattle, we lead people. Lead me, follow me, or get out of my way."

"Better to fight for something than live for nothing."

"Always do everything you ask of those you command."

"Battle is an orgy of disorder."

"If we take the generally accepted definition of bravery as a quality which knows no fear, I have never seen a brave man. All men are frightened. The more intelligent they are, the more they are frightened."

"Wars may be fought with weapons, but they are won by men. It is the spirit of men who follow and of the man who leads that gains the victory."

"Untutored courage is useless in the face of educated bullets."

DWIGHT DAVID 'IKE' EISENHOWER
October 14, 1890 - March 28, 1969

"I hate war as only a soldier who has lived it can, only as one who has seen its brutality, its futility, its stupidity."

"The most terrible job in warfare is to be a second lieutenant leading a platoon when you are on the battlefield."

"We are going to have peace even if we have to fight for it."

"Pessimism never won any battle."

"War settles nothing."

"There is no glory in battle worth the blood it costs."

"In the final choice a soldier's pack is not so heavy as a prisoner's chains."

"It is far more important to be able to hit the target than it is to haggle over who makes a weapon or who pulls a trigger."

"What counts is not necessarily the size of the dog in the fight - it's the size of the fight in the dog."

JULIUS HENRY 'GROUCHO' MARX
October 2, 1890 - August 19, 1977

"Military intelligence is a contradiction in terms."

JULIUS ROBERT OPPENHEIMER
April 22, 1904 - February 18, 1967

"Now I am become death, the destroyer of worlds."

EDWARD TELLER
January 15, 1908 - September 9, 2003

"Had we not pursued the hydrogen bomb, there is a very real threat that we would now all be speaking Russian. I have no regrets."

RONALD REAGAN
February 6, 1911 - June 5, 2004

"People do not make wars; governments do."

"History teaches that war begins when governments believe the price of aggression is cheap."

"No mother would ever willingly sacrifice her sons for territorial gain, for economic advantage, for ideology."

"I call upon the scientific community in our country, those who gave us nuclear weapons, to turn their great talents now to the cause of mankind and world peace: to give us the means of rendering these nuclear weapons impotent and obsolete."

"Of the four wars in my lifetime, none came about because the U.S. was too strong."

"Peace is not absence of conflict; it is the ability to handle conflict by peaceful means."

"A people free to choose will always choose peace."

"Above all, we must realize that no arsenal, or no weapon in the arsenals of the world, is so formidable as the will and moral courage of free men and women. It is a weapon our adversaries in today's world do not have."

"Some people wonder all their lives if they've made a difference. The Marines don't have that problem."

RICHARD NIXON
January 9, 1913 - April 22, 1994

"The greatest honor history can bestow is that of peacemaker."

JOHN FITZGERALD KENNEDY
May 29, 1917 - November 22, 1963

"It is an unfortunate fact that we can secure peace only by preparing for war."

"Forgive your enemies, but never forget their names."

"We have the power to make this the best generation of mankind in the history of the world or to make it the last."

"There is always inequality in life. Some men are killed in a war and some men are wounded and some men never leave the country. Life is unfair."

"Let the word go forth from this time and place, to friend and foe alike, that the torch has been passed to a new generation of Americans - born in this century, tempered by war, disciplined by a hard and bitter peace."

"Those who make peaceful revolution impossible will make violent revolution inevitable."

"Peace is a daily, a weekly, a monthly process, gradually changing opinions, slowly eroding old barriers, quietly building new structures."

"Mankind must put an end to war before war puts an end to mankind."

"Let us never negotiate out of fear. But let us never fear to negotiate."

BILLY GRAHAM
November 7, 1918

"Racism and injustice and violence sweep our world, bringing a tragic harvest of heartache and death."

"Auschwitz stands as a tragic reminder of the terrible potential man has for violence and inhumanity."

ROBERT KENNEDY
November 20, 1925 - June 6, 1968

"Tragedy is a tool for the living to gain wisdom, not a guide by which to live."

MARTIN LUTHER KING JR.
January 15, 1929 - April 4, 1968

"War is a poor chisel to carve out tomorrow."

"The limitation of riots, moral questions aside, is that they cannot win and their participants know it. Hence, rioting is not revolutionary but reactionary because it invites defeat. It involves an emotional catharsis, but it must be followed by a sense of futility."

"It is not enough to say we must not wage war. It is necessary to love peace and sacrifice for it."

"Nonviolence is a powerful and just weapon. Indeed, it is a weapon unique in history, which cuts without wounding and ennobles the man who wields it."

"Nonviolence means avoiding not only external physical violence but also internal violence of spirit. You not only refuse to shoot a man, but you refuse to hate him."

"Man must evolve for all human conflict a method which rejects revenge, aggression and retaliation. The foundation of such a method is love."

"Violence as a way of achieving racial justice is both impractical and immoral. I am not unmindful of the fact that violence often brings about momentary victories. Nations have frequently won their independence in battle. But in spite of temporary victories, violence never brings permanent peace."

"The ultimate measure of a man is not where he stands in moments of comfort and convenience, but where he stands at times of challenge and controversy."

"Means we use must be as pure as the ends we seek."

RON PAUL
August 20, 1935

"What is not conservative about saying, 'Don't go to war unless we go to war properly with a full declaration of war and no other way?'"

"Another term for preventive war is aggressive war - starting wars because someday somebody might do something to us. That is not part of the American tradition."

"There's nothing wrong with being a Conservative and coming up with a conservative belief in foreign policy where we have a strong national defense and we don't go to war so carelessly."

"War is never economically beneficial except for those in position to profit from war expenditures."

GEORGE CARLIN
May 12, 1937 - June 22, 2008

"The very existence of flame-throwers proves that some time, somewhere, someone said to themselves, 'You know, I want to set those people over there on fire, but I'm just not close enough to get the job done.'"

RONALD LEE 'GUNNY' ERMEY
March 24, 1944

"The biggest problem was the politicians knew nothing about fighting a war."

BEN CARSON
September 18, 1951

"What we have to remember is we want to utilize the tremendous intellect that we have in the military to win wars. I've talked to a lot of the generals, a lot of our advanced people. And believe me, if we gave them the mission, which is what the commander-in-chief does, they would be able to carry it out."

"What we have to stop and think about is that we have weakened ourselves militarily to such an extent that it affects all of our military policies."

"There is no such thing as a politically correct war."

DENNIS MILLER
November 3, 1953

"What's so touching is the way we fight the war right until the moment our business is taken care of and then we turn on a dime and we immediately start taking care of people. It's like a shock and aw shucks campaign."

RAND PAUL
January 7, 1963

"The Constitution's pretty clear. The Federalist papers are pretty clear... They very specifically delegated the power to declare war to Congress. They wanted this to be a congressional decision; they did not want war to be engaged in by the executive without approval of Congress."

"No American should be killed by a drone on American soil without first being charged a crime, without first being found guilty of a crime by a court."

"You can't solve a dignity problem with military force."

"The main thing I say on war is that we need to obey the law and formally declare war."

"I believe the answers to most problems that confront us around the world can and should be approached by engaging both friend and foe in dialogue. No, I don't naively think that dialogue always works, but I believe we should avoid the rigidity of saying that dialogue never works."

"Peace through Strength' only works if you have and show strength."

"I tell people I won't vote to go to war unless I'm ready to go or send my kids."

TED CRUZ
December 22, 1970

"The authority to declare war rests in Congress, not in an out-of-control president."

"Is it true that the American people are war-weary? Absolutely. We are tired of sending our sons and daughters to distant lands year after year after year, to give their lives trying to transform foreign nations."

"It's not the job of the U.S. military to do nation-building or produce democratic utopia."

"Leading from behind doesn't work."

THOMAS SOWELL
June 30, 1930

"If you are not prepared to use force to defend civilization, then be prepared to accept barbarism."

"If the battle for civilization comes down to the wimps versus the barbarians, the barbarians are going to win."

"Even the Soviet Union, with its huge nuclear arsenal, was a threat that could be deterred by the prospect of retaliation. But suicide bombers cannot be deterred. They can only be annihilated - preemptively and unilaterally, if necessary."

"Like a baseball game, wars are not over till they are over. Wars don't run on a clock like football. No previous generation was so hopelessly unrealistic that this had to be explained to them."

RICHARD SAMET 'KINKY' FRIEDMAN
November 1, 1944

"I'll keep us out of war with Oklahoma!"

CLINT EASTWOOD
May 31, 1930

"This film cost $31 million. With that kind of money I could have invaded some country."

"The guys who won World War II and that whole generation have disappeared, and now we have a bunch of teenage twits."

"Man becomes his most creative during war."

"A war is a horrible thing, but it's also a unifier of countries."

MARCUS LUTTRELL
November 7, 1975

"Bottom line is that there's bad people everywhere. And every now and again, we are going to have to step to them to make sure that we preserve our way of life."

"There's nothing glorious about war. There's nothing glorious about holding your friends in your arms and watching them die. There's nothing glorious about having to leave your home for 6 to 8 months while your family's back here and you're away."

CHRIS KYLE
April 8, 1974 - February 2, 2013

"War is hell. Hollywood fantasizes about it and makes it look good... war sucks."

"Every time I kill someone, he can't plant an I.E.D. You don't think twice about it."

"It was my duty to shoot the enemy, and I don't regret it. My regrets are for the people I couldn't save: Marines, soldiers, buddies. I'm not naive, and I don't romanticize war. The worst moments of my life have come as a SEAL. But I can stand before God with a clear conscience about doing my job."

"In the end, my story, in Iraq and afterward, is about more than just killing people or even fighting for my country. It's about being a man. And it's about love as well as hate."

"After I was discharged from the military, it was difficult trying to become a civilian."

NORMAN SCHWARZKOPF
August 22, 1934 - December 27, 2012

"As young West Point cadets, our motto was 'duty, honor, country.' But it was in the field, from the rice paddies of Southeast Asia to the sands of the Middle East, that I learned that motto's fullest meaning. There I saw gallant young Americans of every race, creed and background fight, and sometimes die, for 'duty, honor, and their country.'

"It doesn't take a hero to order men into battle. It takes a hero to be one of those men who goes into battle."

"The more you sweat in peace, the less you bleed in war."

"A professional soldier understands that war means killing people, war means maiming people, war means families left without fathers and mothers."

"All you have to do is hold your first soldier who is dying in your arms, and have that terribly futile feeling that I can't do anything about it... Then you understand the horror of war."

"War's a profanity because, let's face it, you've got two opposing sides trying to settle their differences by killing as many of each other as they can."

"I'm not proud of killing, of being responsible for the death of a single person. I never will be."

"I hate war. Absolutely, I hate war."

"Any soldier worth his salt should be antiwar. And still there are things worth fighting for."

V
ON POLITICS

"Whenever you find yourself on the side of the majority, it is time to pause and reflect."- Mark Twain

ABRAHAM LINCOLN
February 12, 1809 - April 15, 1865

"Ballots are the rightful and peaceful successors to bullets."

"To give victory to the right, not bloody bullets, but peaceful ballots only, are necessary."

MARK TWAIN (Samuel Clemens)
November 30, 1835 - April 21, 1910

"The Public is merely a multiplied 'me.'"

"Whenever you find yourself on the side of the majority, it is time to pause and reflect."

THEODORE 'TEDDY' ROOSEVELT
October 27, 1858 - January 6, 1919

"A typical vice of American politics is the avoidance of saying anything real on real issues."

"The most successful politician is he who says what the people are thinking most often in the loudest voice."

WILL ROGERS
November 4, 1879 - August 15, 1935

"Now if there is one thing that we do worse than any other nation, it is try and manage somebody else's affairs."

"Diplomacy is the art of saying 'Nice doggie' until you can find a rock."

"A fool and his money are soon elected."

"I belong to no organized party. I am a Democrat."

"If you ever injected truth into politics you have no politics."

"Anything important is never left to the vote of the people. We only get to vote on some man; we never get to vote on what he is to do."

"Everything is changing. People are taking their comedians seriously and the politicians as a joke."

"There is no more independence in politics than there is in jail."

"The difference between a Republican and a Democrat is the Democrat is a cannibal they have to live off each other, while the Republicans, why, they live off the Democrats."

"Politics has become so expensive that it takes a lot of money even to be defeated."

"The more you observe politics, the more you've got to admit that each party is worse than the other."

ALBERT EINSTEIN
March 14, 1879 - April 18, 1955

"We can't solve problems by using the same kind of thinking we used when we created them."

"The unleashed power of the atom has changed everything save our modes of thinking and we thus drift toward unparalleled catastrophe."

"Only two things are infinite, the universe and human stupidity, and I'm not sure about the former."

"The difference between stupidity and genius is that genius has its limits."

MILTON FRIEDMAN
July 31, 1912 - November 16, 2006

"One man's opportunism is another man's statesmanship."

"Hell hath no fury like a bureaucrat scorned."

DOUGLAS MACARTHUR
January 26, 1880 - April 5, 1964

"One cannot wage war under present conditions without the support of public opinion, which is tremendously molded by the press and other forms of propaganda."

"The world is in a constant conspiracy against the brave. It's the age-old struggle: the roar of the crowd on the one side, and the voice of your conscience on the other."

DWIGHT DAVID 'IKE' EISENHOWER
October 14, 1890 - March 28, 1969

"Politics ought to be the part-time profession of every citizen who would protect the rights and privileges of free people and who would preserve what is good and fruitful in our national heritage."

"Here in America we are descended in blood and in spirit from revolutionists and rebels - men and women who dare to dissent from accepted doctrine. As their heirs, may we never confuse honest dissent with disloyal subversion."

JULIUS HENRY 'GROUCHO' MARX
October 2, 1890 - August 19, 1977

"All people are born alike - except Republicans and Democrats."

"Politics doesn't make strange bedfellows - marriage does."

"Politics is the art of looking for trouble, finding it everywhere, diagnosing it incorrectly and applying the wrong remedies."

ROBERT HEINLEIN
July 7, 1907 - May 8, 1988

"Anyone who considers protocol unimportant has never dealt with a cat."

"Political tags - such as royalist, communist, democrat, populist, fascist, liberal, conservative, and so forth - are never basic criteria. The human race divides politically into those who want people to be controlled and those who have no such desire."

"It is a truism that almost any sect, cult, or religion will legislate its creed into law if it acquires the political power to do so."

EDWARD TELLER
January 15, 1908 - September 9, 2003

"Secrecy, once accepted, becomes an addiction."

RONALD REAGAN
February 6, 1911 - June 5, 2004

"Politics is just like show business. You have a hell of an opening, coast for a while, and then have a hell of a close."

"Politics I supposed to be the second-oldest profession. I have come to realize that it bears a very close resemblance to the first."

"Politics is not a bad profession. If you succeed there are many rewards, if you disgrace yourself you can always write a book."

"I've never been able to understand why a Republican contributor is a 'fat cat' and a Democratic contributor of the same amount of money is a 'public-spirited philanthropist'."

"How do you tell a communist? Well, it's someone who reads Marx and Lenin. And how do you tell an anti-Communist? It's someone who understands Marx and Lenin."

"The trouble with our Liberal friends is not that they're ignorant; it's just that they know so much that isn't so."

"Republicans believe every day is the Fourth of July, but the democrats believe every day is April 15."

"We cannot play innocents abroad in a world that is not innocent."

"We have the duty to protect the life of an unborn child."

"One picture is worth 1,000 denials.

"Facts are stubborn things."

"When you can't make them see the light, make them feel the heat."

RICHARD NIXON
January 9, 1913 - April 22, 1994

"I believe in the battle-whether it's the battle of a campaign or the battle of this office, which is a continuing battle."

"Any change is resisted because bureaucrats have a vested interest in the chaos in which they exist."

"We cannot learn from one another until we stop shouting at one another - until we speak quietly enough so that our words can be heard as well as our voices."

JOHN FITZGERALD KENNEDY
May 29, 1917 - November 22, 1963

"Domestic policy can only defeat us; foreign policy can kill us."

"The ignorance of one voter in a democracy impairs the security of all."

"Let us not seek the Republican answer or the Democratic answer, but the right answer. Let us not seek to fix the blame for the past. Let us accept our own responsibility for the future."

BILLY GRAHAM
November 7, 1918

"Politics has always been ugly to me, and yet I accept that as a fact of life."

"I think where political issues invade moral situations; spiritual leaders have to speak out."

"'Hope and change' has become a cliché in our nation, and it is daunting to think any American could hope for change from what God has blessed."

MARTIN LUTHER KING JR.
January 15, 1929 - April 4, 1968

"When you are right you cannot be too radical; when you are wrong, you cannot be too conservative."

RON PAUL
August 20, 1935

"Well, I don't think we should go to the moon. I think we maybe should send some politicians up there."

"To me, to be a conservative means to conserve the good parts of America and to conserve our Constitution."

GEORGE CARLIN
May 12, 1937 - June 22, 2008

"Just cause you got the monkey off your back doesn't mean the circus has left town."

"If you can't beat them, arrange to have them beaten."

RONALD LEE 'GUNNY' ERMEY
March 24, 1944

"There's a lot of whiners in every crowd."

BEN CARSON
September 18, 1951

"I'm not a politician. I don't want to be a politician, because politicians do what is expedient. I want to do what's right."

"But, you know, we have these entrenched entities - and I'm talking about both Republicans and Democrats - who believe that when you're elected to office, you become some kind of member of the aristocracy, and that anyone who challenges you is attacking you and is unpatriotic. This is foolishness."

"We need to understand that we are not each others' enemies in this country. And it is only the political class that derives power by creating friction. It is only the media that derives its importance by creating friction... that uses every little thing to create this chasm between people. This is not who we are."

FRANKLIN GRAHAM
July 14, 1952

"I've never really been one to try to be politically correct. I just feel truth is truth, and sometimes I probably offend some people."

RAND PAUL
January 7, 1963

"What America needs is not just another politician or more promises. What America needs is a revival."

"The Democrats promised equalizing outcomes through unlimited federal assistance while Republicans offered something that seemed less tangible - the promise of equalizing opportunity through free markets."

"No one politician should be allowed to judge the guilt, to charge an individual, to judge the guilt of an individual and to execute an individual."

"You shouldn't have one opinion when you're running and another when you're president."

"The real debate is, when does life begin? When life begins, it deserves protection."

"I am ready to debate how we fight terrorism without giving up our liberty."

TED CRUZ
December 22, 1970

"There is a liberal fascism that is dedicated to going after believing Christians who follow the biblical teaching on marriage."

"Power in politics, sovereignty in America is with We The People, and that is the path to turning this country around: empowering the people."

"Voters are hungry for principled, conservative fighters - because the threat to our liberties from Washington never has been greater."

"Nobody cares what any politician in Washington says."

"I think most Americans don't really care about politicians bickering in Washington."

THOMAS SOWELL
June 30, 1930

"Liberalism is totalitarianism with a human face."

"People who identify themselves as conservatives donate money to charity more often than people who identify themselves as liberals. They donate more money and a higher percentage of their incomes."

"Socialism in general has a record of failure so blatant that only an intellectual could ignore or evade it."

RICHARD SAMET 'KINKY' FRIEDMAN
November 1, 1944

"The Democrats and Republicans are the same guy admiring themselves in the mirror."

"Politics is the only field in which the more experience you have, the worse you get."

CLINT EASTWOOD
May 31, 1930

"Politicians love regulating. That's part of the whole power structure."
"

"A lot of people are bored of all the political correctness."

"Nowadays, politically, everybody is promising everything. That's the only way you can get elected."

"I would just like to say something, ladies and gentlemen. Something that I think is very important. It is that, you, we - we own this country. We - we own it. It is not you owning it, and not politicians owning it. Politicians are employees of ours."

"If somebody's dumb enough to ask me to go to a political convention and say something, they're going to have to take what they get."

CHRIS KYLE
April 8, 1974 - February 2, 2013

"I am not a fan of politics."

VI

ON FREEDOM OF SPEECH, THE PRESS & CRITICAL THINKING

"Without freedom of thought, there can be no such thing as wisdom - and no such thing as public liberty without freedom of speech."- Benjamin Franklin

BENJAMIN FRANKLIN
January 17, 1706 - April 17, 1790

"He that would live in peace and at ease must not speak all he knows or all he sees."

"As we must account for every idle word, so must we account for every idle silence."

"Any fool can criticize, condemn and complain - and most fools do."

"Words may show a man's wit but actions his meaning."

"He that speaks much is much mistaken."

"Half a truth is often a great lie."

"Remember not only to say the right thing in the right place, but far more difficult still, to leave unsaid the wrong thing at the tempting moment."

"Honesty is the best policy."

"Without freedom of thought, there can be no such thing as wisdom - and no such thing as public liberty without freedom of speech."

GEORGE WASHINGTON
February 22, 1732 - December 14, 1799

"If the freedom of speech is taken away then dumb and silent we may be led, like sheep to the slaughter."

"It is better to offer no excuse than a bad one."

THOMAS PAINE
February 9, 1737 - June 8, 1809

"When men yield up the privilege of thinking, the last shadow of liberty quits the horizon."

"A long habit of not thinking a thing wrong gives it a superficial appearance of being right."

SAMUEL ADAMS
September 27, 1722 - October 2, 1803

"It does not require a majority to prevail, but rather an irate, tireless minority, keen on setting brushfires of freedom in the minds of men."

JAMES MADISON
March 16, 1751 - June 28, 1836

"There is no maxim, in my opinion, which is more liable to be misapplied, and which, therefore, more needs elucidation, than the current one, that the interest of the majority is the political standard of right and wrong."

"The circulation of confidence is better than the circulation of money."

"As long as the reason of man continues fallible, and he is at liberty to exercise it, different opinions will be formed."

"A man has a property in his opinions and the free communication of them."

"A popular government without popular information or the means of acquiring it is but a prologue to a farce, or a tragedy, or perhaps both."

JOHN ADAMS
October 30, 1735 - July 4, 1826

"Facts are stubborn things; and whatever may be our wishes, our inclinations, or the dictates of our passions, they cannot alter the state of facts and evidence."

"Let us tenderly and kindly cherish, therefore, the means of knowledge. Let us dare to read, think, speak, and write."

"Abuse of words has been the great instrument of sophistry and chicanery, of party, faction, and division of society."

THOMAS JEFFERSON
April 13, 1743 - July 4, 1826

"No government ought to be without censors; and where the press is free no one ever will."

"Where the press is free and every man able to read, all is safe."

"Speeches that are measured by the hour will die with the hour."

"I have no fear that the result of our experiment will be that men may be trusted to govern themselves without a master."

"It is error alone which needs the support of government. Truth can stand by itself."

ABRAHAM LINCOLN
February 12, 1809 - April 15, 1865

"There is no grievance that is a fit object of redress by mob law."

"The time comes upon every public man when it is best for him to keep his lips closed."

"I am a firm believer in the people. If given the truth, they can be depended upon to meet any national crisis. The great point is to bring them the real facts."

"Better to remain silent and be thought a fool than to speak out and remove all doubt."

WILLIAM SHERMAN
February 8, 1820 - February 14, 1891

"If I had my choice I would kill every reporter in the world, but I am sure we would be getting reports from Hell before breakfast."

MARK TWAIN (Samuel Clemens)
November 30, 1835 - April 21, 1910

"Never pick a fight with people who buy ink by the barrel."

"Get your facts first, then you can distort them as you please."

"There are lies, damned lies and statistics."

"It usually takes me more than three weeks to prepare a good impromptu speech."

"Only kings, presidents, editors, and people with tapeworms have the right to use the editorial 'we.'"

"The most interesting information comes from children, for they tell all they know and then stop."

"The rule is perfect: in all matters of opinion our adversaries are insane."

"Facts are stubborn, but statistics are more pliable."

"Action speaks louder than words but not nearly as often."

"Let us make a special effort to stop communicating with each other, so we can have some conversation."

THEODORE 'TEDDY' ROOSEVELT
October 27, 1858 - January 6, 1919

"To announce that there must be no criticism of the president... is morally treasonable to the American public."

WILL ROGERS
November 4, 1879 - August 15, 1935

"All I know is just what I read in the papers, and that's an alibi for my ignorance."

"I read about eight newspapers in a day. When I'm in a town with only one newspaper, I read it eight times."

DOUGLAS MACARTHUR
January 26, 1880 - April 5, 1964

"One cannot wage war under present conditions without the support of public opinion, which is tremendously molded by the press and other forms of propaganda."

"Our country is now geared to an arms economy bred in an artificially induced psychosis of war hysteria and an incessant propaganda of fear."

ROBERT HEINLEIN
July 7, 1907 - May 8, 1988

"Never insult anyone by accident."

RONALD REAGAN
February 6, 1911 - June 5, 2004

"Before I refuse to take your questions, I have an opening statement."

"Information is the oxygen of the modern age. It seeps through the walls topped by barbed wire; it wafts across the electrified borders."

JOHN FITZGERALD KENNEDY
May 29, 1917 - November 22, 1963

"A nation that is afraid to let its people judge the truth and falsehood in an open market is a nation that is afraid of its people."

GEORGE CARLIN
May 12, 1937 - June 22, 2008

"By and large, language is a tool for concealing the truth."

BEN CARSON
September 18, 1951

"Quite frankly, having an uninformed populace works extremely well, particularly when you have a media that doesn't understand its responsibility and feels more like it's an arm of a political party. They can really take advantage of an uninformed populace."

DENNIS MILLER
November 3, 1953

"Human beings are human beings. They say what they want, don't they? They used to say it across the fence while they were hanging wash. Now they just say it on the Internet."

TED CRUZ
December 22, 1970

"I am not content to entrust our free-speech rights to the good graces and whims of Congress and hope that politicians don't abuse their power."

THOMAS SOWELL
June 30, 1930

"Both free speech rights and property rights belong legally to individuals, but their real function is social, to benefit vast numbers of people who do not themselves exercise these rights."

CHRIS KYLE
April 8, 1974 - February 2, 2013

"The media cause more problems than they do good."

VII
ON ECONOMICS, CORPORATE & PERSONAL

"So that the record of history is absolutely crystal clear. That there is no alternative way, so far discovered, of improving the lot of the ordinary people that can hold a candle to the productive activities that are unleashed by a free enterprise system."- Milton Friedman

BENJAMIN FRANKLIN
January 17, 1706 - April 17, 1790

"Beware of little expenses. A small leak will sink a great ship."

"A penny saved is two pence clear."

"I am for doing good to the poor, but I differ in opinion about the means. I think the best way of doing good to the poor is not making them easy in poverty, but leading or driving them out of it."

"Our necessities never equal our wants."

"He that's secure is not safe."

"Remember that credit is money."

"Wealth is not his that has it, but his that enjoys it."

"He that has done you a kindness will be more ready to do you another, than he whom you yourself have obliged."

"In this world nothing can be said to be certain, except death and taxes."

"Honesty is the best policy."

"A child thinks 20 shillings and 20 years can scarce ever be spent."

"Time is money."

"A penny saved is a penny earned."

"Creditors have better memories than debtors."

"He that is of the opinion money will do everything may well be suspected of doing everything for money."

"Your net worth to the world is usually determined by what remains after your bad habits are subtracted from your good ones."

"In my youth, I traveled much, and I observed in different countries, that the more public provisions were made for the poor, the less they provided for themselves, and of course became poorer. And, on the contrary, the less was done for them, the more they did for themselves, and became richer."

"Content makes poor men rich; discontent makes rich men poor."

JOHN ADAMS
October 30, 1735 - July 4, 1826

"All the perplexities, confusion and distress in America arise, not from defects in their Constitution or

Confederation, not from want of honor or virtue, so much as from the downright ignorance of the nature of coin, credit and circulation."

THOMAS JEFFERSON
April 13, 1743 - July 4, 1826

"Never spend your money before you have earned it."

ABRAHAM LINCOLN
February 12, 1809 - April 15, 1865

"Labor is prior to, and independent of, capital. Capital is only the fruit of labor, and could never have existed if labor had not first existed. Labor is the superior of capital, and deserves much the higher consideration."

THEODORE 'TEDDY' ROOSEVELT
October 27, 1858 - January 6, 1919

"Probably the greatest harm done by vast wealth is the harm that we of moderate means do ourselves when we let the vices of envy and hatred enter deep into our own natures."

WILL ROGERS
November 4, 1879 - August 15, 1935

"Alexander Hamilton started the U.S. Treasury with nothing, and that was the closest our country has ever been to being even."

"An economist's guess is liable to be as good as anybody else's."

"Money and women are the most sought after and the least known about of any two things we have."

GEORGE WASHINGTON CARVER
c. 1860 - January 5, 1943

"Learn to do common things uncommonly well; we must always keep in mind that anything that helps fill the dinner pail is valuable."

THOMAS EDISON
February 11, 1847 - October 18, 1931

"One might think that the money value of an invention constitutes its reward to the man who loves his work. But... I continue to find my greatest pleasure, and so my reward, in the work that precedes what the world calls success."

HENRY FORD
July 30, 1863 - April 7, 1947

"Wealth, like happiness, is never attained when sought after directly. It comes as a by-product of providing a useful service."

"There is one rule for the industrialist and that is: Make the best quality of goods possible at the lowest cost possible, paying the highest wages possible."

"A business absolutely devoted to service will have only one worry about profits. They will be embarrassingly large."

"Time and money spent in helping men to do more for themselves is far better than mere giving."

"The highest use of capital is not to make more money, but to make money do more for the betterment of life."

"Speculation is only a word covering the making of money out of the manipulation of prices, instead of supplying goods and services."

"It is not the employer who pays the wages. Employers only handle the money. It is the customer who pays the wages."

"The competitor to be feared is one who never bothers about you at all, but goes on making his own business better all the time."

"A market is never saturated with a good product, but it is very quickly saturated with a bad one."

"Business is never so healthy as when, like a chicken, it must do a certain amount of scratching around for what it gets."

"Money is like an arm or leg - use it or lose it."

"It is well enough that people of the nation do not understand our banking and monetary system, for if they did, I believe there would be a revolution before tomorrow morning."

"A business that makes nothing but money is a poor business."

"The man who will use his skill and constructive imagination to see how much he can give for a dollar, instead of how little he can give for a dollar, is bound to succeed."

DOUGLAS MACARTHUR
January 26, 1880 - April 5, 1964

"Our country is now geared to an arms economy bred in an artificially induced psychosis of war hysteria and an incessant propaganda of fear."

HELEN KELLER
June 27, 1880 - June 1, 1968

"It is hard to interest those who have everything in those who have nothing."

"Instead of comparing our lot with that of those who are more fortunate than we are, we should compare it with the lot of the great majority of our fellow men. It then appears that we are among the privileged."

MILTON FRIEDMAN
July 31, 1912 - November 16, 2006

"So that the record of history is absolutely crystal clear. That there is no alternative way, so far discovered, of improving the lot of the ordinary people that can hold a candle to the productive activities that are unleashed by a free enterprise system."

"History suggests that capitalism is a necessary condition for political freedom. Clearly it is not a sufficient condition."

"Most economic fallacies derive from the tendency to assume that there is a fixed pie, that one party can gain only at the expense of another."

"The problem of social organization is how to set up an arrangement under which greed will do the least harm; capitalism is that kind of a system."

"The only way that has ever been discovered to have a lot of people cooperate together voluntarily is through the free market. And that's why it's so essential to preserving individual freedom."

"The black market was a way of getting around government controls. It was a way of enabling the free market to work. It was a way of opening up, enabling people."

"Well first of all, tell me, is there some society you know of that doesn't run on greed? You think Russia doesn't run on greed? You think China doesn't run on greed? What is greed?"

"The most important single central fact about a free market is that no exchange takes place unless both parties benefit."

"Underlying most arguments against the free market is a lack of belief in freedom itself."

DWIGHT DAVID 'IKE' EISENHOWER
October 14, 1890 - March 28, 1969

"We will bankrupt ourselves in the vain search for absolute security."

RONALD REAGAN
February 6, 1911 - June 5, 2004

"I am not worried about the deficit. It is big enough to take care of itself."

"Entrepreneurs and their small enterprises are responsible for almost all the economic growth in the United States."

"Inflation is as violent as a mugger, as frightening as an armed robber and as deadly as a hit man."

"To paraphrase Winston Churchill, I did not take the oath I have just taken with the intention of presiding over the dissolution of the world's strongest economy."

"Recession is when a neighbor loses his job. Depression is when you lose yours."

BILLY GRAHAM
November 7, 1918

"Some people spend their lives building ultimate dream homes so they can enjoy their twilight years... Others spend their last days in nursing homes."

"Give me five minutes with a person's checkbook, and I will tell you where their heart is."

"God has given us two hands, one to receive with and the other to give with."

"Comfort and prosperity have never enriched the world as much as adversity has."

"There is nothing wrong with men possessing riches. The wrong comes when riches possess men."

"Suppose you could gain everything in the whole world, and lost your soul. Was it worth it?"

"If a person gets his attitude toward money straight, it will help straighten out almost every other area in his life."

RON PAUL
August 20, 1935

"A system of capitalism presumes sound money, not fiat money manipulated by a central bank. Capitalism cherishes voluntary contracts and interest rates that are determined by savings, not credit creation by a central bank."

"Of course I've already taken a very modest position on the monetary system; I do take the position that we should just end the Fed."

GEORGE CARLIN
May 12, 1937 - June 22, 2008

"Most people work just hard enough not to get fired and get paid just enough money not to quit."

JAMES MENDEZ JR.
December 04, 1970

"As I drive all over GOD's creation, I have noticed that the poorer the area... the larger the alcohol selection in the convenience store."

BEN CARSON
September 18, 1951

"There is no fulfillment in things whatsoever. And I think one of the reasons that depression reigns supreme amongst the rich and famous is some of them thought that maybe those things would bring them happiness. But what, in fact, does is having a cause, having a passion. And that's really what gives life's true meaning."

"Corporations are not in business to be social-welfare organizations; they are there to make money."

RAND PAUL
January 7, 1963

"I think it's a bad business decision to exclude anybody from your restaurant - but, at the same time, I do believe in private ownership."

"Every debate in Washington is about how much to increase spending - a little or a lot."

"Income inequality is worse in towns run by Democrat mayors than in towns run by Republican mayors."

"What America needs is not Robin Hood but Adam Smith."

"We could try freedom for a while. We had it for a long time. That's where you sell something, and I agree to buy it because I like it. That is how we operate in most of rest of the marketplace other than health care."

"We do not project power from bankruptcy court. We're borrowing a million dollars a minute. It's got to stop somewhere."

"Stop spending money you don't have."

"You campaigned against rich people and you got enough envy whipped up in the country and you're gonna get 'em. You're gonna stick it to those rich people. But guess what? You may not get any more revenue. You may not get any more economic growth. But you can say, 'I stuck it to the rich people.'"

"The great and abiding lesson of American history, particularly the cold war, is that the engine of capitalism, the individual, is mightier than any collective."

"Communism can't survive the captivating allure of capitalism."

TED CRUZ
December 22, 1970

"We ought to be allowing the private sector to pursue every form of energy because the energy of the future, it's not going to come from the government picking winners and losers."

"The reason why I'm a conservative is because conservative policies work and they improve opportunities. They are the avenue for climbing the economic dream."

"We need to conceptualize; we need to articulate conservative domestic policy with a laser focus on opportunity, on easing the means of ascent up the economic ladder."

"The strength of our economy allows us to maintain the mightiest military in the world, effectively enforcing a Pax Americana."

"The American free market system is the greatest engine for prosperity and opportunity that the world has ever seen. Freedom works."

THOMAS SOWELL
June 30, 1930

"The real minimum wage is zero."

"Even if the government spends itself into bankruptcy and the economy still does not recover, Keynesians can always say that it would have worked if only the government had spent more.

RICHARD SAMET 'KINKY' FRIEDMAN
November 1, 1944

"I've always said money may buy you a fine dog, but only love can make it wag its tail."

CLINT EASTWOOD
May 31, 1930

"I do believe in the energy and the productivity of the American business world."

VIII
ON EDUCATION IN THE CITIZENRY

"To educate a man in mind and not in morals is to educate a menace to society."- Theodore Roosevelt

BENJAMIN FRANKLIN
January 17, 1706 - April 17, 1790

"Tell me and I forget. Teach me and I remember. Involve me and I learn."

"I didn't fail the test; I just found 100 ways to do it wrong."

"An investment in knowledge pays the best interest."

"We are all born ignorant, but one must work hard to remain stupid."

"Being ignorant is not so much a shame, as being unwilling to learn."

"The doorstep to the temple of wisdom is a knowledge of our own ignorance."

"The doors of wisdom are never shut."

"Where sense is wanting, everything is wanting."

"By failing to prepare, you are preparing to fail."

"Genius without education is like silver in the mine."

"Hide not your talents. They for use were made. What's a sundial in the shade?"

PATRICK HENRY
May 29, 1736 - June 6, 1799

"I know of no way of judging the future but by the past."

"Fear is the passion of slaves."

GEORGE WASHINGTON
February 22, 1732 - December 14, 1799

"There is nothing which can better deserve your patronage, than the promotion of science and literature. Knowledge is in every country the surest basis of public happiness."

ABIGAIL ADAMS
November 22, 1744 - October 28, 1818

"Learning is not attained by chance; it must be sought for with ardor and diligence."

"If we mean to have heroes, statesmen and philosophers, we should have learned women."

"I've always felt that a person's intelligence is directly reflected by the number of conflicting points of view he can entertain simultaneously on the same topic."

NOAH WEBSTER
October 16, 1758 - May 28, 1843

"In my view, the Christian religion is the most important and one of the first things in which all children, under a free government ought to be instructed."

"It is the sincere desire of the writer that our citizens should early understand that the genuine source of correct republican principles is the Bible, particularly the New Testament or the Christian religion."

JAMES MADISON
March 16, 1751 - June 28, 1836

"A well-instructed people alone can be permanently a free people.

"War contains so much folly, as well as wickedness, that much is to be hoped from the progress of reason."

"If we are to take for the criterion of truth the majority of suffrages, they ought to be gotten from those philosophic and patriotic citizens who cultivate their reason."

"Knowledge will forever govern ignorance; and a people who mean to be their own governors must arm themselves with the power which knowledge gives."

"Learned Institutions ought to be favorite objects with every free people. They throw that light over the public mind which is the best security against crafty and dangerous encroachments on the public liberty."

"The advancement and diffusion of knowledge is the only guardian of true liberty."

JOHN ADAMS
October 30, 1735 - July 4, 1826

"Let us tenderly and kindly cherish, therefore, the means of knowledge. Let us dare to read, think, speak, and write."

"Liberty cannot be preserved without general knowledge among the people."

"I must study politics and war that my sons may have liberty to study mathematics and philosophy."

THOMAS JEFFERSON
April 13, 1743 - July 4, 1826

"Politics is such a torment that I advise everyone I love not to mix with it."

"Enlighten the people generally, and tyranny and oppressions of body and mind will vanish like evil spirits at the dawn of day."

"To penetrate and dissipate these clouds of darkness, the general mind must be strengthened by education."

"I know of no safe depository of the ultimate powers of the society but the people themselves; and if we think them not enlightened enough to exercise their control with a wholesome discretion, the remedy is not to take it from them but to inform their discretion."

"I cannot live without books."

"Whenever the people are well-informed, they can be trusted with their own government."

ABRAHAM LINCOLN
February 12, 1809 - April 15, 1865

"Upon the subject of education, not presuming to dictate any plan or system respecting it, I can only say that I view it as the most important subject which we, as a people, can be engaged in."

"Let reverence for the laws be breathed by every American mother to the lisping babe that prattles on her lap - let it be taught in schools, in seminaries, and in colleges; let it be written in primers, spelling books, and in almanacs; let it be preached from the pulpit, proclaimed in legislative halls, and enforced in courts of justice."

"A capacity, and taste, for reading gives access to whatever has already been discovered by others."

"Books serve to show a man that those original thoughts of his aren't very new at all."

"For my part, I desire to see the time when education - and by its means, morality, sobriety, enterprise and industry - shall become much more general than at present, and should be gratified to have it in my power to contribute something to the advancement of any measure which might have a tendency to accelerate the happy period."

"The philosophy of the school room in one generation will be the philosophy of government in the next."

ROBERT EDWARD LEE
January 19, 1807 - October 12, 1870

"The education of a man is never completed until he dies."

MARK TWAIN (Samuel Clemens)
November 30, 1835 - April 21, 1910

"I never let schooling interfere with my education."

"Ideally a book would have no order to it, and the reader would have to discover his own."

"Education consists mainly of what we have unlearned.

"Be careful about reading health books. You may die of a misprint."

"It ain't what you don't know that gets you into trouble. It's what you know for sure that just ain't so."

"The difference between the almost right word and the right word is really a large matter - 'tis the difference between the lightning-bug and the lightning."

"'Classic.' A book which people praise and don't read."

"A person who won't read has no advantage over one who can't read."

"Everything has its limit - iron ore cannot be educated into gold."

THEODORE 'TEDDY' ROOSEVELT
October 27, 1858 - January 6, 1919

"To educate a man in mind and not in morals is to educate a menace to society."

"A thorough knowledge of the Bible is worth more than a college education."

WILL ROGERS
November 4, 1879 - August 15, 1935

"There's only one thing that can kill the movies, and that's education."

"There is nothing so stupid as the educated man if you get him off the thing he was educated in."

"There are three kinds of men. The one that learns by reading. The few who learn by observation. The rest of them have to pee on the electric fence for themselves."

"Why don't they pass a constitutional amendment prohibiting anybody from learning anything? If it works as well as prohibition did, in five years Americans would be the smartest race of people on Earth."

GEORGE WASHINGTON CARVER
c. 1860 - January 5, 1943

"Education is the key to unlock the golden door of freedom."

THOMAS EDISON
February 11, 1847 - October 18, 1931

"Genius is one percent inspiration and ninety-nine percent perspiration."

HENRY FORD
July 30, 1863 - April 7, 1947

"You can't learn in school what the world is going to do next year."

HELEN KELLER
June 27, 1880 - June 1, 1968

"College isn't the place to go for ideas."

"People do not like to think. If one thinks, one must reach conclusions. Conclusions are not always pleasant."

"Literature is my Utopia. Here I am not disenfranchised. No barrier of the senses shuts me out from the sweet, gracious discourses of my book friends. They talk to me without embarrassment or awkwardness."

"Knowledge is love and light and vision."

MILTON FRIEDMAN
July 31, 1912 - November 16, 2006

"Universities exist to transmit knowledge and understanding of ideas and values to students not to provide entertainment for spectators or employment for athletes."

DWIGHT DAVID 'IKE' EISENHOWER
October 14, 1890 - March 28, 1969

"Don't join the book burners. Do not think you are going to conceal thoughts by concealing evidence that they ever existed."

JULIUS HENRY 'GROUCHO' MARX
October 2, 1890 - August 19, 1977

"I must say I find television very educational. The minute somebody turns it on, I go to the library and read a good book."

"Outside of a dog, a book is a man's best friend. Inside of a dog it's too dark to read."

JULIUS ROBERT OPPENHEIMER
April 22, 1904 - February 18, 1967

"No man should escape our universities without knowing how little he knows."

ROBERT HEINLEIN
July 7, 1907 - May 8, 1988

"Don't handicap your children by making their lives easy."

JOHN ARCHIBALD WHEELER
July 9, 1911 - April 13, 2008

"We live on an island surrounded by a sea of ignorance. As our island of knowledge grows, so does the shore of our ignorance."

JOHN FITZGERALD KENNEDY
May 29, 1917 - November 22, 1963

"Our progress as a nation can be no swifter than our progress in education. The human mind is our fundamental resource."

"The greater our knowledge increases the more our ignorance unfolds."

"A child miseducated is a child lost."

"The goal of education is the advancement of knowledge and the dissemination of truth."

BILLY GRAHAM
November 7, 1918

"Every human being is under construction from conception to death."

MARTIN LUTHER KING JR.
January 15, 1929 - April 4, 1968

"The function of education is to teach one to think intensively and to think critically. Intelligence plus character - that is the goal of true education."

"Rarely do we find men who willingly engage in hard, solid thinking. There is an almost universal quest for easy answers and half-baked solutions. Nothing pains some people more than having to think."

GEORGE CARLIN
May 12, 1937 - June 22, 2008

"I went to a bookstore and asked the saleswoman,'Where's the self-help section?' She said if she told me, it would defeat the purpose."

RONALD LEE 'GUNNY' ERMEY
March 24, 1944

"I firmly believe that you live and learn, and if you don't learn from past mistakes, then you need to be drug out and shot."

BEN CARSON
September 18, 1951

"Our schools too often want to shut people up so they can't talk about real solutions. People who think differently tend to clam up because they think something is wrong with their ideas."

"Intelligent people tend to talk about the facts. They don't sit around and call each other names. That's what you can find on a third grade playground."

"If you go and talk to most people, they mean well but they don't have much of a breadth on education, of knowledge of understanding what the real issues are and therefore they listen to pundits on television who tell them what they are supposed to think and they keep repeating that until pretty soon they say, 'Oh, well that must be true.'"

"With everything that is complex, we learn. If you don't learn, then it's an utter and abject failure. If you do learn, and you're able to apply that to the next situation, then you take away a measure of success."

"Education is a fundamental principle of what made America a success. We can't afford to throw any young people away."

DENNIS MILLER
November 3, 1953

"You know there is a problem with the education system when you realize that out of the 3 R's only one begins with an R."

"The American education system couldn't be more badly directed or poorly funded if the Secretary of Education were Ed Wood."

RAND PAUL
January 7, 1963

"The government can't even do a good job of something as simple as running the Post Office. How can it be expected to do a good job with something really important, like educating our children?"

"When you look at statistics for the white community alone, you see that we've become two separate worlds in which the successful are educated and wait to have children until they are married, and those in poverty are primarily those without higher education and with children outside of marriage."

"Every child in every neighborhood, of every color, class and background, deserves a school that will help them succeed."

TED CRUZ
December 22, 1970

"School choice is the civil rights issue of the 21st century."

THOMAS SOWELL
June 30, 1930

"Those parts of history that would undermine the vision of the Left - which prevails in our education system from elementary school to postgraduate study - are not likely to get much attention."

"Creating whole departments of ethnic, gender, and other 'studies' was part of the price of academic peace. All too often, these 'studies' are about propaganda rather than serious education."

"Education is not merely neglected in many of our schools today, but is replaced to a great extent by ideological indoctrination."

"Just what is it that academics have to fear if they stand up for common decency, instead of letting campus barbarians run amok?"

"Too much of what is called 'education' is little more than an expensive isolation from reality."

"It takes considerable knowledge just to realize the extent of your own ignorance.

"Our schools and colleges are turning out people who cannot feel fulfilled unless they are telling other people what to do."

"The march of science and technology does not imply growing intellectual complexity in the lives of most people. It often means the opposite."

"The problem isn't that Johnny can't read. The problem isn't even that Johnny can't think. The problem is that Johnny doesn't know what thinking is; he confuses it with feeling."

**RICHARD SAMET 'KINKY' FRIEDMAN
November 1, 1944**

"The teachers are getting screwed, blued, and tattooed by the system."

"I'll tell you right now. I'm for prayer in school."

JOHN WAYNE
May 26, 1907 - June 11, 1979

"Life is tough, but it's tougher if you're stupid."

ORVILLE WRIGHT
August 19, 1871 - January 30, 1948

"If we all worked on the assumption that what is accepted as true is really true, there would be little hope of advance."

WILBUR WRIGHT
April 16, 1867 - May 30, 1912

"Men become wise just as they become rich, more by what they save than by what they receive."

CHUCK NORRIS
March 10, 1940

"In America the schools have become too permissive, the kids now are controlling the schools, the tail is wagging the dog. We've got to make a change there and get it back to where the teachers have control of the classrooms."

"I think you can learn from history."

GEORGE EASTMAN
July 12, 1854 - March 14, 1932

"The progress of the world depends almost entirely upon education."

RICHARD BUCKMINSTER 'BUCKY' FULLER
July 12, 1895 - July 1, 1983

"What usually happens in the educational process is that the faculties are dulled, overloaded, stuffed and paralyzed so that by the time most people are mature they have lost their innate capabilities."

"You can never learn less, you can only learn more."